Philip Allan
Publishers

# A-Level

## Exam

# ics

## Questions
## Choice

## *Sheila Garrett*

# Titles available

## A-Level

Physics: Structured Questions & Multiple Choice

Biology: Essays

British History, 1815–1951

Business Studies: Essays

Chemistry: Multiple Choice

Chemistry: Structured Questions & Essays

Computing

Economics: Data Response

Economics: Essays

Economics: Multiple Choice

English: Practical Criticism

European History, 1789–1945

French

Geography: Essays

History: Europe of the Dictators, 1914–1945

Law: General Principles

Media Studies

Politics: Essays

Pure Mathematics

Religious Studies: The New Testament — The Gospels

Religious Studies: The Philosophy of Religion

Sociology: Essays

Philip Allan Publishers Limited
Market Place
Deddington
Oxfordshire OX15 0SE

Telephone: 01869 338652

© Philip Allan Publishers Limited 1998

Formerly published by Richard Ball Publishing
Revised 1998

ISBN 0 86003 305 8

This is a revised (and combined) edition of *A-Level Physics: 16 Comprehensive Tests* and *A-Level Physics: 8 Multiple Choice Tests* published by Richard Ball Publishing in 1994.

Typeset and illustrated by Magnet Harlequin, Oxford and printed by Information Press, Eynsham, Oxford

# Contents

| | | Questions | Answers |
|---|---|---|---|
| | Introduction | | |
| 1 | Mechanics | 3 | 91 |
| 2 | Momentum and energy | 8 | 97 |
| 3 | Circular motion, rotation and gravitation | 12 | 102 |
| 4 | Simple harmonic motion | 16 | 107 |
| 5 | Materials | 21 | 112 |
| 6 | Geometric optics and progressive waves | 25 | 117 |
| 7 | Wave properties | 30 | 122 |
| 8 | Temperature and internal energy | 35 | 129 |
| 9 | Using thermal energy | 39 | 133 |
| 10 | Gases | 45 | 139 |
| 11 | Current electricity | 50 | 146 |
| 12 | Magnetic effects of electricity | 55 | 156 |
| 13 | Electric and gravitational fields | 60 | 162 |
| 14 | Capacitors | 64 | 167 |
| 15 | Radioactivity | 69 | 175 |
| 16 | Atomic processes | 73 | 181 |
| 17 | Units and graphs | 78 | 188 |
| 18 | Revision | 83 | 193 |

# Acknowledgements

Many thanks to my whole family for their support and help. I would also like to thank colleagues from Cambridge Tutors College who have helped with the computing. Any criticism, suggestions and notification of errors would be much appreciated. I am grateful to London Examinations, a division of Edexcel Foundation, for permission to reproduce questions from past examination papers. Edexcel Foundation, London Examinations accepts no responsibility whatsoever for the accuracy or method of working in the answers given.

# Introduction

This Exam Success Guide has been written to help you pass A- or A/S-level Physics and can be used for any syllabus. You can use it throughout your course as well as in the run up to your examination to help you revise. For ease of reference the book is set out in test modules, but topics can be selected in any order. The fully-worked answers provided at the back of the book show how to gain full marks in descriptive questions as well as in calculations.

There are 18 tests altogether, each designed to take 1 hour 20 minutes. They all have two sections: Section 1 contains structured questions while Section 2 includes multiple choice (useful for quick revision). Select the test you want. Find a quiet, comfortable, well-lit place to work, set a timer and get started. When you have finished, you can turn to the back of the Guide to check your answers. Read descriptive answers particularly carefully to make sure you have included everything, otherwise you could lose valuable marks. If you are not satisfied with your efforts, try the same test again the following week. Your confidence will increase and so will your chance of success!

# Some Useful Tips

### During the course
(a) You have chosen A-level Physics — you need to pass!
(b) You must become actively involved in the subject, so add your own notes and explanations to those you are given.
(c) Read magazines and newspaper articles about satellites, space and other scientific topics. This will enhance your general understanding.
(d) Write a project on some aspect of Physics outside your syllabus. Are you interested in astronomy, particle physics, meteorology, geophysics or medical applications?
(e) Use your formula sheet (if you are allowed one) all the time so you become completely acquainted with it.

### Revising for the examination
(a) Make yourself a timetable which finishes about one week before the examinations commence.
(b) Select your least favourite topic to start.
(c) Keep to the timetable. Do not repeat those topics you find easy.
(d) Become actively involved in your revision. Do lots of writing, draw diagrams, sketch graphs, etc.
(e) Make a set of cards which summarise your notes. You can refer to these for quick revision at any time.

### Just before the examination
(a) Check your timetable with other students, particularly the times of exams as well as their dates. There is always someone who gets it wrong!
(b) Make a list of everything you need for each exam.

(c) Make any purchases at least one week before you want to use them.

(d) Check the length of each paper. How many questions are you expected to answer? Is there any choice?

**For the examination itself**

(a) Check the contents of your bag against your prepared list.

(b) Have a good night's sleep.

(c) Arrive early.

# Words Used in Physics Examinations

Have you been told to 'read the question'? Almost certainly the answer is 'yes'. Questions asked in Physics examinations use many of the following words. Make sure you know exactly what they mean.

(a) DEFINE requires a precise and complete definition. Do not use symbols unless you say what they represent. Word definitions are usually acceptable. Make a list of all the definitions you are expected to know.

(b) DESCRIBE an experiment means exactly what it says. A labelled diagram is essential together with a clear statement of what to do (in the correct order), including any necessary graphs and calculations.

(c) EXPLAIN requires a sequence of events, related to well-known laws. It needs logical statements, following on from one another.

(d) ESTIMATE usually requires a number. Always try! For example, estimate the diameter of a baby's head. What would you write?

(e) DRAW/SKETCH — you will have practised these. Include as many diagrams as possible in all your answers (well labelled, of course).

(f) ASSUMPTION is often designed to make life more simple, e.g. assume no drag, assume constant temperature, etc. Always look for something obvious.

(g) LIST means make a list, perhaps of measurements. Include units if possible.

(h) QUALITATIVE means explain in words only. Numbers are not expected.

(i) QUANTITATIVE means numbers definitely are required.

(j) CALCULATE — quote a formula, perhaps, and then use it. Be careful with units and significant figures.

(k) THEORY is an idea which usually backs up an experiment, e.g. kinetic theory.

(l) CONCLUSION requires a clear final statement of your discovery.

# A-Level
# Physics

questions

# Test 1
## Mechanics

Time allowed: *1 hour 20 minutes*

## Section 1: Short Questions

**QUESTION**

**1**

(a) An object dropped from an aircraft flying at a height of 5 km accelerates until it reaches a terminal speed. Write down an expression for the resultant downward force on the object before it reaches the terminal speed.

By applying Newton's Second Law of Motion to the falling object, explain its behaviour.

(b) A small ball of plasticine is released on the surface of water in the cylinder shown on the right and allowed to fall. The time intervals $t_1$, $t_2$, $t_3$ and $t_4$ taken for the ball to fall between the equally-spaced levels marked in the diagram are then carefully measured. Explain how you would decide from the measurements whether or not the ball had achieved its terminal speed.

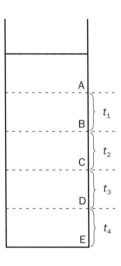

Describe how you would measure the terminal speed assuming it had been achieved before the ball reached level C.

**2**

A box of mass 40 kg rests on a flat horizontal surface. It is subjected to a constant horizontal force of 200 N and a maximum frictional force of 120 N. Draw a free body diagram of the box showing all four forces that act on it. Indicate the magnitude of each force. Write down the magnitude and the direction of the resultant force on the box.

How far will the box move from rest in 4.0 s?

**3**

In an experiment to measure the acceleration of free fall, a steel ball took 807 ms to fall a distance of 3.20 m from rest. Calculate a value for the acceleration of free fall.

The uncertainty in the time of fall was ± 5 ms. What is the percentage uncertainty in the value of the acceleration you have just calculated?

**QUESTION**

**4**

The diagrams below show a sphere, S, resting on a table and a free-body diagram on which the forces acting on the sphere have been marked.

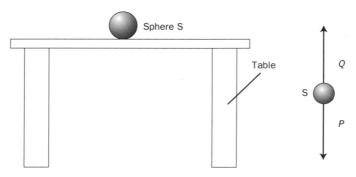

We know from Newton's Third Law of Motion that forces occur in equal and opposite pairs.

On which body does the force which pairs with $P$ act? Give its direction.

On which body does the force which pairs with $Q$ act? Give its direction.
A force $F_1$ acts on an object O and this same force $F_1$ forms a Newton's Third Law pair with a second force, $F_2$. State two ways in which $F_1$ and $F_2$ are similar and two ways in which they differ.

**5**

A squash ball is dropped from rest on to a bench and bounces back to half the original height. Draw a velocity–time graph for its motion ignoring air resistance.
Use the graph to explain:

**(a)** Where the ball hits the bench.
**(b)** What happens to the acceleration of the ball.
**(c)** How you could find the distance the ball rises.

**6**

This is a velocity–time graph for a car with a mass of 1000 kg. It is travelling along a straight road.

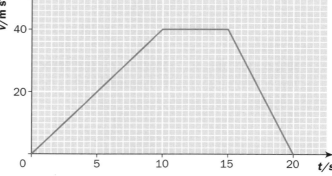

**(a)** How far does it go altogether?
**(b)** What is the momentum of the car when it reaches maximum speed?
**(c)** What is the acceleration of the car during the first 10 s?
**(d)** What is the constant resultant accelerating force during this 10 s?
**(e)** The car is moving through the air, so the total driving force will not be the same as calculated in **(d)**. Sketch a graph to show how the driving force varies with time during this time interval.

**QUESTION**

**7**

State Newton's Second Law of Motion. Describe an experiment to show how you would investigate the relationship between force and acceleration in the laboratory.

## Section 2: Multiple Choice

*Select one answer only for each question.*

**1**

An object falls through air under the influence of the earth's gravitational field. Which graph best represents the variation of acceleration $a$ with time $t$?

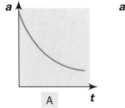 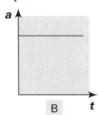 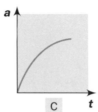  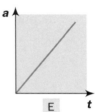

**2**

The force which accelerates a car forwards is:

.........................................................

A   The force of the car on the road.
B   The force of friction on the road.
C   The push of the road on the car.
D   The force of the engine on the car.
E   The weight of the car.

**3**

A constant force $F$ accelerates a given mass $m$ from rest through a given distance. The velocity it gains is proportional to:

.........................................................

A   $m$
B   $m^{1/2}$
C   $1\ m^{-1/2}$
D   $1\ m^{-1}$
E   $1\ m^{-2}$

**4**

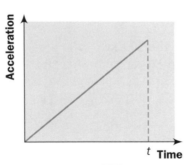

The graph shows the variation of acceleration with time for a body undergoing linear motion. The area under the graph measures:

.........................................................

A   Distance travelled.
B   Average acceleration up to time $(t)$.
C   Average velocity up to time $(t)$.
D   Impulse given to the body.
E   Velocity at time $(t)$.

In a tug of war match the teams are exactly balanced. The pull of one team is 800 N.

**5**

The tension in the rope (in N) is:

A  800
B  400
C  0
D  1600
E  1000

**6**

The pull of the other team (in N) is:

A  800
B  400
C  0
D  1600
E  1000

**7**

A man stands on bathroom scales in a lift. The mass of the man is 75 kg. What will the scales read (in N) if the lift accelerates upwards at 5 m s$^{-2}$?

A  50
B  375
C  0
D  760
E  1125

**8**

Two masses 6 kg and 4 kg are connected together by a light string running over a frictionless pulley. If the inclined plane is smooth, the acceleration of the system (in m s$^{-2}$) is:

A  10
B  1
C  0.1
D  2
E  5

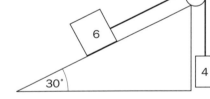

**9**

What force $F$ will just raise the 100 kg load at a constant speed (in N)?

A  1000
B  101
C  10
D  100
E  0

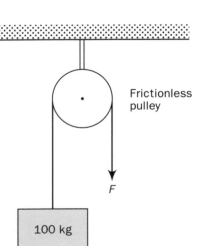

Frictionless pulley

$F$

100 kg

**QUESTION**

**10**

An object is dropped from a landing module as it approaches the moon. The module is travelling at a steady velocity of 10 m s$^{-1}$ and is 100 m above the moon when this occurs. If the moon's gravitational acceleration is 1.6 m s$^{-2}$, at what speed (m s$^{-1}$) does the object hit the moon?

| | |
|---|---|
| A | 320 |
| B | 420 |
| C | 17.9 |
| D | 20.5 |
| E | 10.0 |

## Momentum and energy

Time allowed: *1 hour 20 minutes*

## Section 1: Short Questions

**QUESTION 1**

Distinguish between *elastic* and *inelastic* collisions.

For each of the following examples, state (1) whether the collision is elastic or inelastic, and (2) what energy changes occur, if any.

**(a)** A bullet becoming embedded in a stationary target.
**(b)** A gas molecule colliding with another gas molecule.
**(c)** A beta-particle having an ionising collision with an air molecule.

**2**

In an alpha particle scattering experiment, a particular alpha particle collides head-on with a gold nucleus in a sheet of gold foil, and rebounds. Sketch a velocity–time graph showing how the velocity of the alpha particle changes during the collision. The graph should start and end when the alpha particle is some distance from the gold nucleus.

Mark clearly on the graph the point at which the acceleration of the alpha particle has its maximum value.

**3**

A ball of mass 0.16 kg moving at a speed of 35 m s$^{-1}$ is struck by a bat and travels away from the bat in the opposite direction to that of its approach. What is the momentum of the ball before being struck?

The graph below shows the force which acts on the ball during its period of contact $t_1 t_2$ with the bat.

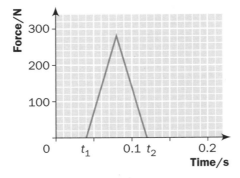

Calculate:
**(a)** The average force applied to the ball during its contact with the bat.
**(b)** The impulse applied to the ball.
**(c)** The speed of the ball after it has been struck by the bat.

**QUESTION**

**4**

A block of wood (mass 1.5 kg) hangs on a piece of string. A bullet (mass 50 g) is fired at a speed of 88 m s$^{-1}$ into the block and stays inside. The block swings up to one side.

(a) What type of collision is this?
(b) Is the momentum conserved?
(c) Is kinetic energy conserved?
(d) What was the kinetic energy of the bullet before it entered the block?
(e) What was the momentum of the bullet before it entered the block?
(f) What is the speed of the block with the bullet inside after the collision?
(g) How high does the block rise?

**5**

A small child is sitting in the rear seat of a car not wearing a seat belt. The driver is wearing a seat belt. The driver suddenly stops the car. The driver is not injured but the child is thrown forward. Use the principles of physics to explain why this happened. What features of car design help to reduce forces in a crash?

**6**

An electron of mass $9.0 \times 10^{-31}$ kg is travelling at $10^6$ m s$^{-1}$. Calculate:

(a) The kinetic energy of the electron.
(b) The momentum of the electron.

Are these quantities vector or scalar? What is the difference between a vector and a scalar quantity?

Give two more examples of each.

**7**

(a) State the Law of Conservation of Momentum.
(b) An experiment was carried out to investigate the different types of collision.

Trolley A (mass 1.6 kg) collided with trolley B (mass 0.8 kg)
The speed of A before the collision was 0.6 m s$^{-1}$.
The speed of A after the collision was 0.37 m s$^{-1}$.

The speed of B before the collision was 0.10 m s$^{-1}$.
The speed of B after the collision was 0.57 m s$^{-1}$.

Make calculations to show that momentum was conserved and identify the type of collision.

# Test 2

## Section 2: Multiple Choice

*Select one answer only for each question.*

**1** Which of the following is true for an elastic collision?

| | Total energy | Momentum | Kinetic energy |
|---|---|---|---|
| A | conserved | conserved | not conserved |
| B | not conserved | not conserved | not conserved |
| C | conserved | conserved | conserved |
| D | not conserved | conserved | not conserved |
| E | conserved | not conserved | conserved |

**2** A ball bearing free falls on to a horizontal metal plate and rebounds to exactly the same height. Which of the following is true?

A It is an inelastic collision.
B It is an elastic collision.
C Most of its energy is dissipated as sound and heat.
D The ball does not undergo a change in momentum.
E The ball's velocity is constant.

**3** A trolley of mass 100 g is given a velocity of 6 m s$^{-1}$. The kinetic energy of the trolley (in J) is:

A 1.8
B 0.3
C 1800
D 300
E 30

**4** Energy transferred can be calculated directly from:

A force × velocity.
B pressure × change in volume.
C force × acceleration.
D mass × acceleration.
E mass × velocity.

**5** A car travelling along a level road at a speed of 10 m s$^{-1}$ crashes head on into a wall. If the mass of the car is 1000 kg then the kinetic energy and momentum before collision are:

| | Kinetic energy (J) | Momentum (kg m s$^{-1}$) |
|---|---|---|
| A | $5 \times 10^3$ | $10 \times 10^4$ |
| B | $5 \times 10^4$ | $5 \times 10^3$ |
| C | $5 \times 10^4$ | $1 \times 10^4$ |
| D | $1 \times 10^5$ | $5 \times 10^3$ |
| E | $5 \times 10^3$ | $1 \times 10^4$ |

**QUESTION**

**6**

A steady stream of balls, each of mass 0.4 kg, hits a vertical wall at right angles. If the speed of the balls is 15 m s$^{-1}$ and 600 hit the wall every 10 s rebounding at the same speed, then the average force acting on the wall is (in N):

A  12
B  72
C  360
D  720
E  7200

**7**

A stationary uranium nucleus suddenly disintegrates to an isotope of thorium (mass 234) with the emission of an alpha particle (mass 4). The ratio: (speed of alpha particle)/(speed of thorium nucleus) is:

A  4/234
B  234/4
C  $(4/234)^2$
D  $(234/4)^2$
E  58.5

**8**

If $p$ is the momentum of an object mass $m$ then $p^2/m$ has the same units as:

A  m s$^{-2}$
B  J s$^{-1}$
C  N s
D  N
E  J

**9**

Four railway trucks are all linked together and standing on a track. Each has the same mass $m$. Another truck with mass $2m$ is moving at 5 m s$^{-1}$. It collides with the stationary trucks and links with them. After the collision all the trucks move off together with a speed (in m s$^{-1}$) of:

A  5/2
B  5/3
C  5/4
D  5/5
E  5/6

**10**

A motor uses electrical energy at a rate of 1000 W. It is used to raise a block of 200 N. The block moves 16 m in 4 s. The percentage efficiency of the motor is:

A  12.8%
B  20.0%
C  80.0%
D  96%
E  100%

# Test 3

## Circular motion, rotation and gravitation

**Time allowed:** *1 hour 20 minutes*

## Section 1: Short Questions

**QUESTION**

**1**

An ice skater of mass 70 kg moves across an ice rink with speed 7.0 m s⁻¹ along a circular path of radius 10 m.

**(a)** Draw a free body diagram showing the forces which act on the skater. Mark on the diagram the position of the centre of the circular path.

**(b)** Explain, with reference to this example, the term *centripetal force* and calculate its magnitude in this instance.

**2**

In the diagram AB represents the raised bonnet of a car, hinged freely at A. The bonnet is of mass 12 kg and its weight acts through the point G.

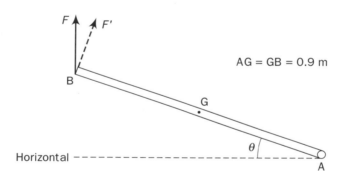

AG = GB = 0.9 m

**(a)** Calculate the value of the vertical force *F* that will just maintain the position of the bonnet.

**(b)** Instead of applying a vertical force to raise the bonnet, a force *F′* is applied perpendicular to the surface of the bonnet.

  **(i)** Calculate *F′* for *θ* = 24°.

  **(ii)** Hence explain why it is easier to raise the bonnet by applying a force in the direction of *F* than by applying a force in the direction of *F′*.

**3**

The gravitational force acting on an astronaut travelling in a space vehicle in low earth orbit is only slightly less than if he was standing on earth.

**(a)** Explain why the force is only slightly less.

**(b)** Explain why, when travelling in the space vehicle, the astronaut appears to be 'weightless'.

**QUESTION**

**4**

A spacecraft on its way to the moon is first placed in a circular orbit around the earth. In this orbit the radius is approximately 6560 km, and the acceleration due to gravity is 9.4 m s$^{-2}$. Calculate:

(a) The speed of the spacecraft.
(b) The time for one complete revolution.

**5**

Robert (R), mass 20 kg, hangs vertically on a rope suspended from a branch in a tree.

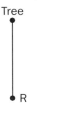
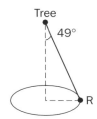

What is the tension in the rope?

He then swings in a horizontal circular path of radius 3.0 m. He does not touch the ground. What is the tension in the rope now?

**6**

(a) An aeroplane is travelling horizontally at a constant velocity.
    Draw a diagram to show the four main forces acting on the aeroplane.
    Explain the origin of each of the forces.
(b) The aircraft now turns into a circular path. What force provides the centripetal acceleration?

**7**

An object of mass 2.0 kg on the end of a piece of string is whirled in a vertical circle at a constant speed of 5.0 m s$^{-1}$. If the diameter of the circle is 4.0 m, what are the maximum and minimum tensions in the string? Where do they occur?

# Section 2: Multiple Choice

*Select one answer only for each question.*

**1**

A satellite of mass $m$ circles the earth with speed $v$. It remains at a constant distance $d$ from the centre of the earth. Which of the following statements is true? The satellite has:

A   Acceleration towards the centre of the earth of $mv^2/d$.
B   Time period of $2\pi d/v$.
C   Constant velocity.
D   Speed $2v$ in orbit of radius $2d$.
E   Time period of $v/2d$.

# Test 3

**2–3**

The time the earth takes to go once round the sun is 365 days. Mean radius of orbit is $1.5 \times 10^8$ km.

**2**

What is the average speed of the earth?

A  300 km s$^{-1}$
B  $8.0 \times 10^{-17}$ m s$^{-1}$
C  $6.0 \times 10^{-2}$ m s$^{-1}$
D  $3.0 \times 10^4$ m s$^{-1}$
E  600 km s$^{-1}$

**3**

What is the acceleration of the earth towards the sun (in m s$^{-2}$)?

A  $2.0 \times 10^7$
B  $6.0 \times 10^3$
C  $2.0 \times 10^{-7}$
D  $6.0 \times 10^{-3}$
E  $3.0 \times 10^{-3}$

**4**

A satellite moves in a circular orbit around the earth. This motion is best described by:

A  Speed varying: acceleration constant.
B  Speed constant: acceleration constant.
C  Force constant: speed varying.
D  Velocity constant: acceleration zero.
E  Velocity constant: acceleration constant.

**5–6**

The two forces shown act on a cylinder of radius 20 cm.

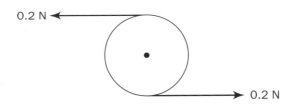

**5**

The torque acting on the cylinder is (in N m):

A  0.04
B  0.16
C  0.40
D  0.80
E  0.08

**6**

The work done (J) as the cylinder rotates once is:

A 0.03
B 0.25
C 1.00
D 0.05
E 0.50

**7**

A girl whirls a conker on the end of a string so that it moves in a horizontal circle. The conker moves at constant speed. Which of the following statements is incorrect:

A The conker is pulled towards the girl.
B The string pulls the conker in towards the centre.
C The string pulls the girl's hand outwards.
D The conker is not travelling at constant velocity.
E If the string is cut the velocity will immediately change.

**8**

A body is moving in a circle of radius 10 m at constant speed. The time period is 5 s. Its acceleration towards the centre of the circle is:

A $16.0\pi^2$
B $1.6\pi^2$
C $1.6\pi$
D $0.4\pi$
E $0.4\pi^2$

**9**

A mass of 2 kg travels round in a horizontal circle. The radius of the circle is 5 m and the time for one complete revolution is 4 s. The force acting on the mass (in N) is:

A $(5/2)\pi^2$
B $\pi$
C $\pi^2/2$
D $8\pi^2$
E $(5/4)\pi^2$

**10**

A body is moving in circular motion with a uniform angular speed 0.6 rad s$^{-1}$ and a uniform linear speed of 3.0 m s$^{-1}$. The radial acceleration (in m s$^{-2}$) is:

A 0
B 0.2
C 1.8
D 3.0
E 18.0

# Test 4
## Simple harmonic motion

**Time allowed:** *1 hour 20 minutes*

## Section 1: Short Questions

**QUESTION**

**1**

**(a)** Define simple harmonic motion.
**(b)** State four situations in which this motion occurs.
**(c)** Sketch a graph to show how displacement varies with time.

**2**

Sketch graphs to show how the following quantities vary with displacement during simple harmonic motion:

**(a)** acceleration;
**(b)** velocity;
**(c)** kinetic energy.

**3**

A mass of 0.4 kg, hanging from the end of a light spring, extends it by 0.31 m. The mass is then pulled down a further 0.06 m and released, causing it to execute vertical oscillations that are simple harmonic. Calculate the frequency of the oscillations.

The motion of the mass is described on the displacement–time graph shown below.

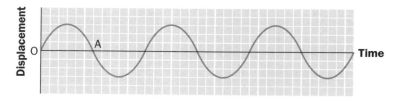

**(a)** What is the value of the amplitude of the motion?
**(b)** Calculate the displacement per small scale division on the vertical axis of the graph, if it is to correctly represent the motion of the mass.
**(c)** What length of time is represented by the distance OA marked on the graph?

**QUESTION**

**4**

The graph below shows how the speed, $v$, of a pendulum bob varies with time, $t$.

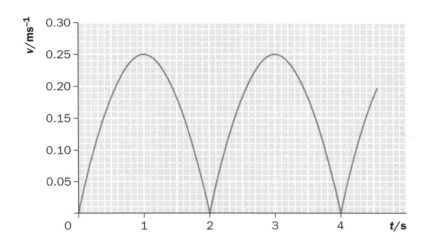

(a) Use this speed–time graph to find the amplitude of the motion of the bob.
(b) Find the average speed of the bob during the first 4 s.
(c) What is the average velocity of the bob over the first 4 s?

Explain your answer.

**5**

A particle has a mass of 100 g and is performing simple harmonic motion with amplitude 20 mm. The largest force at any one time is $6.4 \times 10^{-2}$ N. Find a value for:

(a) maximum velocity;
(b) time for one complete oscillation.

**6**

A simple pendulum can be used to measure time. What is meant by a simple pendulum?

Find the length of a simple pendulum which could be used to measure seconds on the surface of the earth (take $g = 9.8 \text{ m s}^{-2}$).

What would happen to the time period of this pendulum if it was taken to the moon, where $g = 1.6 \text{ m s}^{-2}$?

**7**

Describe an experiment to show that the motion of a pendulum is approximately simple harmonic.

## Section 2: Multiple Choice

*Select one answer only for each question.*

**1**

A simple pendulum of length $l$ has a time period $T$ on the surface of the earth. What is its time period on the surface of the moon? (Acceleration of free fall on moon $= g/6$.)

A  $3T$
B  $6T$
C  $\sqrt{3}\,T$
D  $\sqrt{6}\,T$
E  $1/6T$

**2–3**

A particle performs simple harmonic motion with amplitude 2.0 cm and time period 0.10 s.

**2**

Its maximum velocity (in cm s$^{-1}$) is:

A  20
B  126
C  63
D  252
E  200

**3**

Its velocity 1.0 cm from centre (in cm s$^{-1}$) is:

A  63
B  109
C  100
D  252
E  200

**4**

Which diagram shows the forces acting on a pendulum bob when it is at maximum displacement?

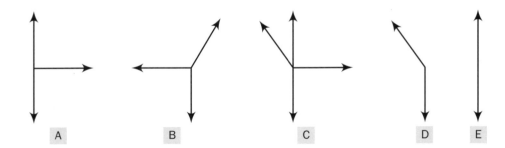

A      B      C      D      E

**QUESTION**

**5**

A simple pendulum oscillates with simple harmonic motion. If different lengths (L) give rise to different periodic times (T) then a graph of log L against log T will have a slope equal to:

A $^1/_2$
B 2
C $\sqrt{2}$
D $1/\sqrt{2}$
E $-1/2$

**6**

When an object undergoes simple harmonic motion the phase difference between its acceleration and displacement is (in radians):

A 0
B $\pi/4$
C $\pi/2$
D $3\pi/4$
E $\pi$

**7**

For a particle executing simple harmonic motion, which of these pairs of quantities will have their minimum values at the same instant?

A Acceleration and kinetic energy.
B Kinetic energy and potential energy.
C Velocity and potential energy.
D Acceleration and displacement.
E Velocity and acceleration.

**8 – 10**

Study this graph of simple harmonic motion.

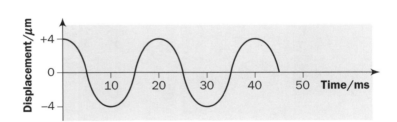

**8**

The frequency of the vibration (in Hz) is:

A 1000
B 100
C 50
D 10
E 1

**9**

The amplitude of the vibration (in $\mu$m) is:

A 2
B 4
C 6
D 8
E 20

The maximum velocity of the
vibration (in $\mu$m s$^{-1}$) is:

A   $1600\pi$
B   $800\pi$
C   $400\pi$
D   $40\pi$
E   $20\pi$

# Test 5
## Materials

**Time allowed:** *1 hour 20 minutes*

## Section 1: Short Questions

**QUESTION**

**1**

A large tensile force is needed to increase the length of a steel wire by about 0.1%, but a modest tensile force doubles the length of a rubber band. Explain how the difference in behaviour is accounted for by the different molecular structures of steel and rubber.

Explain why, if a steel wire is formed into a helical spring, the amount of elastic potential energy it can store increases enormously.

**2**

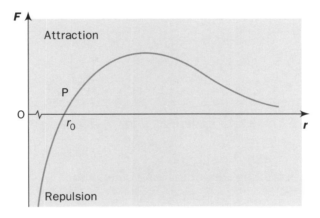

The graph shows how the force, $F$, between a pair of molecules might vary with their separation, $r$. Describe in words how the force, $F$, between a pair of molecules varies:
**(a)** as $r$ decreases from the value $r_0$;
**(b)** as $r$ increases from the value $r_0$.

What is the significance of the separation value $r_0$?

**3**

**(a)** What stress would produce a strain of 0.0002
  **(i)** in a strip of steel;
  **(ii)** in a strip of polythene?
**(b)** Sketch a stress–strain graph for both steel and polythene using the same set of axes.
**(c)** A steel wire has a length of 2 m and a diameter of 2.0 mm. What extension is produced if a load of 10 N is suspended at one end?
**(d)** A strip of polythene has a cross-section measuring 1.0 cm by 0.2 mm. What strain is produced if the load is suspended from this strip?

Young's modulus for steel is $2.0 \times 10^{11}$ Pa and for polythene $3.0 \times 10^7$ Pa.

**QUESTION**

**4**

A spring of length 80 cm is suspended from a clamp stand. The spring extends 10 mm when a load of 10 g is added to the bottom. The 10 g mass is then pulled down a further 5 mm and then released. If the oscillation of the spring is simple harmonic, calculate:

(a) The time period.
(b) The maximum velocity of the mass.
(c) The kinetic energy of the mass as it passes through the centre of the motion.

**5**

Explain why:

(a) It is difficult to extend a metal bar.
(b) It is difficult to compress a metal bar.

**6**

A steel wire is suspended vertically and weights are slowly added at the bottom until the wire breaks.

Sketch a force–extension graph for the wire and use it to explain:

(a) the elastic region;
(b) the plastic region;
(c) the breaking point;
(d) the yield point;
(e) the significance of the area under the graph.

**7**

You are asked to find Young's modulus for a steel wire.

(a) Define Young's modulus.
(b) Draw a labelled diagram of the apparatus.
(c) List the measurements you would make.
(d) Show how you would use these to find Young's modulus for steel.

# Section 2: Multiple Choice

*Select one answer only for each question.*

**1**

A copper wire of radius $r$ supports a load and is found to have a strain of $12 \times 10^{-5}$. A second copper wire of the same length but of radius $2r$ supports exactly the same load. The strain for the second wire is:

A  $3 \times 10^{-5}$
B  $6 \times 10^{-5}$
C  $12 \times 10^{-5}$
D  $36 \times 10^{-5}$
E  $48 \times 10^{-5}$

**QUESTION**

**2**

Which of the following has no units?

A  Strain.
B  Stress.
C  Density.
D  Velocity.
E  Speed.

**3**

A load of 15 N produces an extension of 0.1 mm in a wire 10 m long. If the diameter of the wire is 3.2 mm then an approximate value (in $N\,m^{-2}$) for Young's modulus is:

A  $1.9 \times 10^5$
B  $1.9 \times 10^8$
C  $1.9 \times 10^{11}$
D  $3.0 \times 10^8$
E  $9.4 \times 10^5$

**4**

A long copper wire, fixed at the top, is subjected to a load hanging at the lower end. The extension could be increased by:

A  Using a shorter wire.
B  Decreasing the load.
C  Increasing the load.
D  Increasing the diameter.
E  Using a wire with a larger value of Young's modulus.

**5**

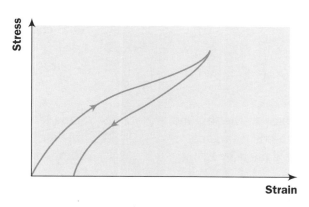

A sample of rubber was subjected to a force that was slowly increased from zero and then decreased back to zero. The above graph was obtained. Which of the following statements is true?

A  When the load is applied and removed energy is dissipated in the rubber.
B  Young's modulus stays constant.
C  The sample returns to its original length.
D  The rubber breaks.
E  The slope of the graph can be used to calculate the energy stored in the rubber.

QUESTION

**6**

During an experiment to find Young's modulus for a wire, a graph of stress against strain was plotted.
If $W$ is the force applied,
   $L$ is the original length of the wire,
   $A$ is the area of cross-section,
   $e$ is the extension of the wire,
which of these graphs should be plotted?

A  $W/e$ against $L/A$.
B  $W/A$ against $L/e$.
C  $We$ against $AL$.
D  $WL$ against $Ae$.
E  $W/A$ against $e/L$.

**7**

Wire A is suspended vertically with load $m$ at its lower end. Wire B is also suspended vertically with the same load. Wire B is twice as long as A and twice the diameter of A. If the elastic limit is not exceeded, then the ratio extension of A/extension of B is:

A  4
B  2
C  1
D  0.5
E  0.25

**8**

Which of the following has the same units as pressure?

A  Strain.
B  Energy stored per unit volume.
C  Total energy stored.
D  Load.
E  Extension.

**9**

A copper wire is fixed at the top and its extension measured. A larger extension could be gained by using:

A  Same length of steel wire.
B  Smaller load on the same wire.
C  Thinner copper wire.
D  Shorter copper wire.
E  Decrease the temperature.

**10**

Two wires of different materials are extended by the same amount by equal loads. They are the same length. The thinner wire has diameter $d$ and Young's modulus $E$.
The thicker wire has diameter $2d$.
What is Young's modulus for the thicker wire?

A  $4E$
B  $2E$
C  $E$
D  $E/4$
E  $E/2$

# Test 6

## Geometric optics and progressive waves

**Time allowed:** *1 hour 20 minutes*

## Section 1: Short Questions

**1**

A narrow parallel beam of white light strikes the mid-point of the side of a 60° prism at an angle of incidence greater than 30°. Draw a diagram showing what happens to the light as it passes into the prism and out of the far side.

Explain, with references to your diagram, the meaning of the terms refraction, deviation and dispersion.

**2**

What is meant by a progressive wave?

The water on one side of a ripple tank is deeper than the other side. The dividing line is XY. On the deeper side the wave speed of the ripples is $0.26 \text{ m s}^{-1}$. On the shallower side the wave speed is $0.20 \text{ m s}^{-1}$. What is the critical angle for these waves? Make a sketch to show the apparatus you would use to demonstrate refraction of water waves.

**3**

Explain the meaning of the following terms. Use diagrams if possible.

**(a)** Multimode optical fibre.
**(b)** Step index optical fibre.
**(c)** Attenuation of the signal.

**4**

The absolute refractive index of air is 1.00. The absolute refractive index of glass is 1.50. Plot a graph to show the variation of:

**(a)** angle of refraction $\theta_2$ against angle of incidence $\theta_1$
     (as angle of incidence varies from 0 to 90°);
**(b)** $\sin \theta_1$ against $\theta_2$.

**5**

**(a)** Explain the difference between longitudinal and transverse waves.
**(b)** Name three examples of each.
**(c)** A tiny source P is emitting waves which can be detected by an aerial A. A meter which is connected to the aerial measures the intensity of the waves. At first the distance PA = $d$. When this distance is increased to $2d$ the meter reading falls to one quarter of its initial value. Explain why.

**QUESTION**

**6**

Visible light and microwaves both belong to the same spectrum.

(a) What is the name of this spectrum?
(b) Which of these radiations has the shorter wavelength?
(c) Name two properties they have in common.
(d) Describe an experiment you could do to show microwaves are reflected.

**7**

Explain the difference between mechanical waves and electromagnetic waves. Name two different types of mechanical waves and explain how they could be demonstrated in the laboratory.

# Section 2: Multiple Choice

*Select one answer only for each question.*

**1**

Which of the following is the correct sequence for electromagnetic waves in order of decreasing frequency?

A   Microwaves, radio, red light, $\gamma$ rays.
B   Microwaves, blue light, ultraviolet, radio.
C   X-rays, ultraviolet, infra-red, radio.
D   X-rays, blue light, radio, microwaves.
E   $\gamma$ rays, red light, blue light, radio.

**2**

A wave of frequency 10 Hz travels through a medium at 5 m s$^{-1}$. At any instant the minimum separation (in m) between two points at which the displacement is zero is:

A   4.00
B   2.00
C   1.00
D   0.50
✓ E   0.25

*[handwritten:]*
$f = 10Hz$  $c = 5ms^{-1}$
* minimum separation between two points at which the displacement is zero
↳ minimum separation where displacement = 0
i.e. half of wave length
using $c = f\lambda$ 2) $\lambda = \frac{5}{10} = 0.5$
but that half $\lambda = 0.25m$

**3**

A sound wave of frequency 200 Hz is travelling at a speed of 320 m s$^{-1}$.
Two points on the wave that are 0.4 m apart will be out of phase by:

A   $\pi$
✓ B   $\pi/2$
C   $\pi/4$
D   $3\pi/4$
E   $4\pi/3$

*[handwritten:]*
$c = f\lambda$
$320 = 200\lambda \Rightarrow \lambda = 1.6$
$\lambda \sim 2\pi$
$0.4 \sim x$
$x = \frac{0.4 \times 2\pi}{1.6}$
$= \frac{\pi}{2}$

OR using phase difference $= \frac{2\pi}{\lambda} \times$ path difference
$= \frac{2\pi \times 0.4}{1.6}$
$= \frac{\pi}{2} //$

**QUESTION**

**4**

Which of the following statements about waves is true?

✗ A  Sound waves can be polarised.

✗ B  Sound waves cannot interfere destructively.

✗ C  Longitudinal waves cannot be diffracted.

✓ D  Electromagnetic waves can be diffracted.

✗ E  Stationary waves are always transverse.

**5**

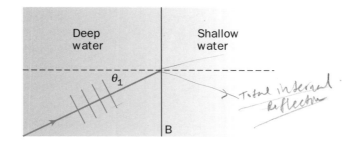

A water wave approaches a boundary B dividing the deep water from the shallow water. $\theta_1$ is the angle between the direction of the original wave and the normal.

$V_1$ is the speed of the wave in the deep water. If $\theta_2$ is the angle between the direction of the refracted wave and the normal and $V_2$ is the speed of the wave in the shallow water, then:

A  Total internal reflection could occur in the deeper water.

B  $\theta_1 < \theta_2$

C  $\theta_1 > \theta_2$

D  $V_1 < V_2$

E  $V_1 = V_2$

**6**

In the electromagnetic spectrum which of these shows the way characteristics change on moving from X-rays to infra-red?

✗ A  Frequency remains constant; wavelength increases.

✓ B  Speed in vacuo is constant; wavelength increases.

✗ C  Speed in vacuo is constant; wavelength decreases.

✗ D  Speed in vacuo decreases; wavelength decreases.

✗ E  Speed in vacuo increases; wavelength increases.

# Test 6

**7**

Which of these shows that light is a transverse, rather than a longitudinal, wave motion?

A   Light is refracted by a block of glass.
B   Light obeys the inverse square law.
✓ C   Light is polarised by reflection from glass.
D   Light is diffracted by a diffraction grating.
E   Light beams interfere in Young's slits experiment.

**8**

When light travels from air into perspex the radiation experiences:

A   Change in frequency but not in speed or wavelength.
B   Change in frequency, wavelength and speed.
C   Change in frequency and speed but not in wavelength.
✓ D   Change in wavelength and speed but not in frequency.
E   Change in wavelength but not in speed.

**9**

Light travels through a hemispherical glass block along the path IPT.

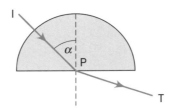

The critical angle at P is *c*. If α is:

✓ A   Bigger than *c* then no light is transmitted.
B   Smaller than *c* then no light is transmitted.
C   Zero then all the light is reflected.
D   Smaller than *c* then no light is reflected.
E   Bigger than *c* then no light is reflected.

**QUESTION**

**10**

A spherical air bubble is trapped inside a glass block. How will this affect the path of a light ray travelling through the block? When the incoming light ray hits the bubble, which path will it take?

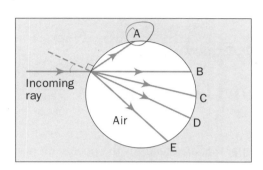

# Test 7

## Wave properties

**Time allowed:** *1 hour 20 minutes*

## Section 1: Short Questions

**1**

Sketch a diagram of apparatus arranged for the observation of the interference pattern produced in Young's two slits experiment. State suitable values for the relevant dimensions.

Explain the parts played by diffraction and by the principle of superposition in accounting for:

**(a)** The overall width of the pattern.
**(b)** The alternation of bright and dark bands within the pattern.

**2**

Light from a cadmium discharge lamp can be used to determine the spacing of the lines on a plane diffraction grating. This is done by measuring the angle $\phi$ between the diffracted beams either side of the normal in the first order spectrum for light incident normally on the grating.

**(a)** If the measured value of $\phi$ is 46° 43' and the red line used in the cadmium spectrum is of wavelength 644 nm, calculate the number of lines per metre on the grating.
**(b)** Make a suitable calculation to test whether the second-order spectrum of this line will be visible.

**3**

What is meant by simple harmonic motion? A wire of mass per unit length $5.0 \text{ g m}^{-1}$ is stretched between two points 30 cm apart. The tension in the wire is 70 N.
Calculate the frequency of the sound emitted by the wire when it oscillates in its fundamental mode. Explain, with reference to this example, the term 'damped harmonic motion'.

**4**

The diagram shows a parallel beam of light incident upon a flat transparent solid surface of refractive index $n$. The light is both reflected and refracted.

Brewster's Law states that the reflected light is wholly plane polarised when the angle of incidence is $\theta_p$ where $\tan \theta_p = n$.

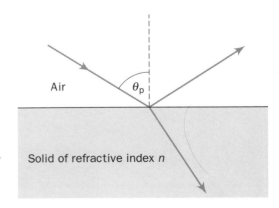

**(a)** What do you understand by plane polarised light?
**(b)** Describe briefly how you would try to verify Brewster's Law in the laboratory.

**QUESTION**

**5**

**(a)** A ripple tank can be used to demonstrate wave properties. How would you use it to show interference?

**(b)** How could you show interference using microwaves?

**6**

A sound wave can be formed by a vibrating object. Explain the meaning of the terms:

**(a)** Velocity of a wave.

**(b)** Wavelength of a wave.

**(c)** The diagram shows two loudspeakers connected to a single source. The waves are picked up by a microphone. Explain how the sound intensity varies along the line XY. You may assume the wavelength of the sound is small compared with the distances involved.

**7**

Explain how you would set up a stationary wave on a stretched string. Give a labelled diagram of the apparatus you would use. Why is it called 'stationary'?

## Section 2: Multiple Choice

*Select one answer only for each question.*

**1**

A stretched string is plucked and gives a fundamental frequency $f$. The length of the string and the tension are both halved. The new fundamental frequency will be:

A   $2\sqrt{2}\, f$

B   $\sqrt{2}\, f$

C   $f$

D   $f/\sqrt{2}$

E   $f/2$

QUESTION

2

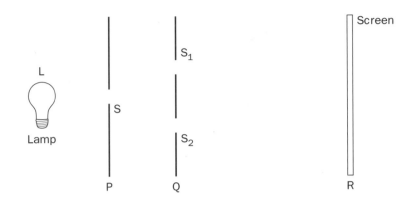

The above diagram shows the apparatus for Young's two slit experiment. A series of fringes is observed on the screen.

The separation of these fringes can be decreased by:

A  Replacing L by a monochromatic source of smaller wavelength.

B  Moving screen P closer to Q.

C  Increasing width of slit S.

D  Decreasing the distance between $S_1$ and $S_2$.

E  Moving the screen Q further away from R.

3

This question is about progressive and stationary waves. The table below gives information about these two types of waves. Which one of these statements is not necessarily true?

|   |   | Progressive wave | Stationary wave |   |
|---|---|---|---|---|
| A | Displacement of particles is: | parallel | perpendicular | to direction of energy travel |
| B | Adjacent particles in the wave are: | out of | in | phase with each other |
| C | Frequencies of particles in the wave: | are | are not | the same |
| D | Amplitudes of particles in the wave: | are | are not | the same |
| E | Energy: | is | is not | transferred along the wave |

## QUESTION

**4**

All waves can be:

A  Plane polarised and reflected.
B  Plane polarised and refracted.
C  Plane polarised but not refracted.
D  Plane polarised but not reflected.
E  Reflected but not plane polarised.

**5**

Monochromatic light of wavelength $6.0 \times 10^{-7}$ m falls normally on to a diffraction grating having 600 lines $mm^{-1}$. The angular position of the second-order spectrum on one side of the normal is:

A  46°
B  23°
C  21°
D  13°
E  1°

**6**

A mechanical wave of frequency 300 Hz travels along a metal railway line at 6000 m s$^{-1}$. Two points on the rail which are 2.5 m apart are out of phase by:

A  0
B  $\pi$
C  $\pi/2$
D  $\pi/4$
E  $\pi/8$

**7**

Two matching sources produce waves with wavelength $\lambda$. When the two waves meet they have a phase difference of $\pi/2$ radians. The path difference could be:

A  $2\lambda$
B  $\lambda$
C  $\lambda/2$
D  $\lambda/4$
E  $3\lambda/4$

**8**

Two steel wires of the same length are stretched horizontally under the same tension. If the wires have radii 2.0 mm and 1.0 mm and fundamental frequencies of $f_1$ and $f_2$, respectively, then:

A  $f_1 = f_2$
B  $f_1 = \sqrt{2}\, f_2$
C  $f_2 = 4f_1$
D  $2f_2 = f_1$
E  $2f_1 = f_2$

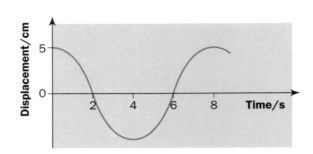

The above shows a displacement–time graph for an oscillator.

**9**

At what times (in seconds) is the speed of the oscillator zero?

- A   2 and 6.
- B   4 and 8.
- C   0 and 2.
- D   2 and 4.
- E   2 and 8.

......................................................

**10**

Which of these statements is NOT true when time $t = 2$ s?

- A   Speed is maximum.
- B   Acceleration is maximum.
- C   Kinetic energy is maximum.
- D   Potential energy is zero.
- E   Displacement is zero.

......................................................

# Temperature and internal energy

**Time allowed:** *1 hour 20 minutes*

## Section 1: Short Questions

**QUESTION**

**1**

The distance between the 0°C mark and the 100°C mark on a mercury-in-glass thermometer is 20.0 cm. How far from the 0°C mark will the mercury be if the temperature is:

(a) +16.0°C;
(b) –5.0°C.

**2**

The First Law of Thermodynamics states
$$\Delta U = \Delta Q + \Delta W$$

(a) What is another name for this equation?
(b) Explain the meaning of each of the three terms.
(c) If a system is at constant temperature, which of these three quantities would have a value of zero?

**3**

A thermometer uses a physical property to measure temperature. Name three different types of thermometer and in each case explain which physical property is used.

**4**

(a) What is meant by the term 'thermal equilibrium'?
(b) How do you recognise that a thermocouple junction has reached thermal equilibrium?
(c) Give an example in which a thermocouple would be preferable to a mercury-in-glass thermometer.
(d) State three advantages of the thermocouple in your given situation.

**5**

The First Law of Thermodynamics can be applied to an electric light bulb that has been switched on for some time and has reached a steady temperature. Explain the meaning of the following three terms in this case:
$$\Delta U \quad \Delta Q \quad \Delta W$$

**QUESTION**

**6**

An electrical resistance thermometer uses a piece of platinum wire to measure temperature. The resistance of the wire is $3.500\,\Omega$ at the ice point and $3.780\,\Omega$ at the steam point. At an unknown temperature its resistance is $3.620\,\Omega$. What is this unknown temperature? Does the electrical resistance thermometer have any advantages over the mercury-in-glass thermometer in some situations?

**7**

Explain how you would use a thermocouple to measure the temperature of a beaker of oil in the laboratory. Your description should include:

**(a)** How you would calibrate the thermometer.
**(b)** What measurements you would take.
**(b)** How you would calculate the unknown temperature.

## Section 2: Multiple Choice

*Select one answer only for each question.*

**1**

In a thermometer, the length of mercury thread is 200 mm above the bulb when the bulb is placed in steam at 100°C. The length changes to 48 mm when in water at 20°C. What is the length (in mm) in water at 0°C?

A   0
B   40
C   38
D   10
E   20

**2**

Which of the following graphs illustrates the relationship between the internal energy $U$ of an ideal gas and the temperature $T$ of the gas (in K)?

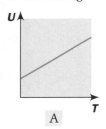 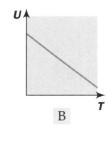 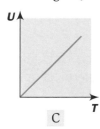 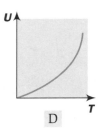 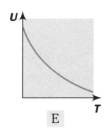

A      B      C      D      E

**3**

The average energy of an atom in a solid at temperature $T$ (in Kelvin) is $3\,kT$ where $k$ is Boltzmann's constant ($k = 1.38 \times 10^{-23}$ J K$^{-1}$). The average energy of a copper atom (in J) at a temperature of 300 K is:

A   1.24
B   $1.24 \times 10^{-20}$
C   $12.4 \times 10^{-20}$
D   $414 \times 10^{-20}$
E   $4.14 \times 10^{-21}$

**QUESTION**

**4**

The First Law of Thermodynamics implies that:

A   Internal energy is conserved.
B   Momentum is conserved.
C   Energy is conserved.
D   Temperature remains constant.
E   No heat flows in or out of the system.

**5**

The First Law of Thermodynamics states

$$\Delta U = \Delta Q + \Delta W$$

where
$\Delta U$ is the change in internal energy of the system,
$\Delta Q$ is thermal energy transferred, and
$\Delta W$ is work done on the system.

If a real gas undergoes an isothermal expansion:

A   $\Delta W = \Delta U$
B   $\Delta Q = \Delta U$
C   $\Delta W = 0$
D   $\Delta U = 0$
E   $\Delta Q = 0$

**6**

For an ideal gas the net change in its internal energy is zero if it is:

A   Allowed to expand but no heat enters or leaves.
B   Heated at constant volume so the pressure increases.
C   Allowed to expand, heat is supplied and the temperature remains the same.
D   Allowed to expand, heat is supplied and the pressure remains the same.
E   Cooled at constant volume.

**7**

Which of the following instruments would you use to detect infra-red waves?

A   Geiger counter.
B   Electrometer.
C   Loudspeaker.
D   Thermopile.
E   Microphone.

When measuring the temperature at the bottom of a very deep pond, which of the following is NOT true?

A  You could use an electrical resistance thermometer.

B  You could use a thermocouple.

C  The thermometer and the water must be in thermal equilibrium.

D  You could use a mercury-in-glass thermometer.

E  The thermometer should have a large thermal capacity.

9

A copper-constantan thermocouple with its cold junction at 0°C has an e.m.f. of 5.00 mV when its hot junction is at 100°C.

What is the reading of the e.m.f. in volts if the hot junction is at 60°C?

A  $2.0 \times 10^{-3}$

B  $2.0 \times 10^{-4}$

C  $3.0 \times 10^{-3}$

D  $3.0 \times 10^{3}$

E  $3.0 \times 10^{4}$

10

A thermometer is required to measure a rapidly changing temperature. Which of these properties is NOT important?

A  Good thermal contact.

B  Quick response.

C  Low thermal capacity.

D  High thermal capacity.

E  High sensitivity.

# Test 9
## Using thermal energy

Time allowed: *1 hour 20 minutes*

## Section 1: Short Questions

QUESTION
1

The diagrams show a power transistor attached to a finned, dull-black, metal heat sink. Describe how the thermal energy flows from the transistor to the surroundings and indicate the design features which keep the thermal energy flow rate high.

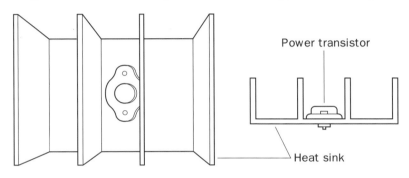

2

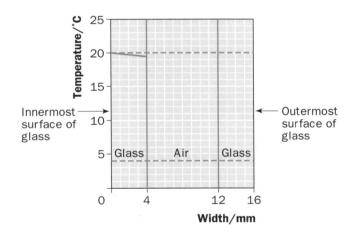

The incomplete diagram above shows how the temperature changes across a double-glazed window unit. Each pane of glass is 4 mm thick and the air gap is 8 mm. The temperature of the innermost surface of the glass is 20°C and of the outermost surface is 4°C. Copy the diagram on to graph paper and complete it to show how the temperature falls across the air gap and the outer pane of glass.

Use the diagram to calculate the average temperature gradient across the whole unit. If the power transfer per unit area is 120 W m$^{-2}$, what is the 'equivalent' thermal conductivity of the unit as a whole?

QUESTION

3

A layer of fibreglass, 100 mm thick, covers an area of 40 m² in the roof space of a house. In winter the temperature in the roof space just above the layer of fibreglass is 6°C and the temperature of the plasterboard surface supporting the fibreglass is 18°C. If the thermal conductivity of the fibreglass is 0.04 W m⁻¹K⁻¹, what is the power loss through the fibreglass?

What would be the effect of doubling the thickness of the layer of fibreglass?
What would be the advantage of having the fibreglass layer during a hot summer?

4

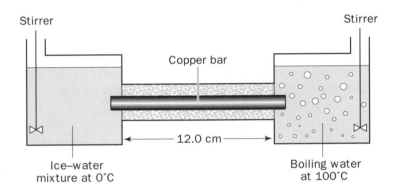

The diagram shows a lagged copper bar acting as a thermal link between a bath of boiling water and an ice–water mixture.

Calculate the energy flow per second through the bar. Hence calculate the mass of ice which should melt during a 15 s period. Write down one important assumption you make.

In practice the amount of ice that melts per second is likely to be different from the calculated amount. Give a reason why the calculated amount might be:

(a) higher, and
(b) lower

than the amount melted in practice. Thermal conductivity of copper = 385 W m⁻¹ K⁻¹, area of cross-section of copper bar = 1.50 cm², specific latent heat (specific enthalpy change) of fusion of ice = 3.34 × 10⁵ J kg⁻¹.)

5

A car has one metal disc attached to each of its four wheels. The discs are used to brake the car. Each disc has a mass of 3.0 kg and specific heat capacity of 500 J kg⁻¹ K⁻¹. Calculate:

(a) the heat capacity of four discs
(b) the temperature rise of one disc

if the car is travelling at 40 m s⁻¹ when the brakes are applied to stop the car. The mass of the car is 1000 kg.

QUESTION
6

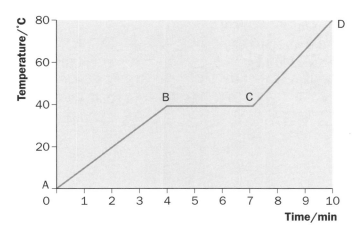

The diagram shows a temperature–time graph as 1 kg of a solid is heated uniformly at a rate of 2000 J min⁻¹.

**(a)** Explain what is happening to the molecules of the material during the separate periods of time AB, BC and CD.
**(b)** Explain why the temperature stays constant from B to C.
**(c)** Calculate the specific heat capacity of the solid (use A–B).
**(d)** Calculate the latent heat of fusion of the material (use B–C).

7

Describe an experiment to measure the heat capacity of a metal calorimeter. Make sure you give:

**(a)** a labelled diagram;
**(b)** measurements made;
**(c)** calculations.

## Section 2: Multiple Choice

*Select one answer only for each question.*

1

A slab of material P is 2 mm thick and is placed in good thermal contact with a piece of material Q which is 20 mm thick. The cross-sectional areas of P and Q are the same, but the thermal conductivity of Q is 40 times that of P. If the outer surface of P is at 100°C and the outer surface of Q is at 0°C, then the temperature of the common interface is:

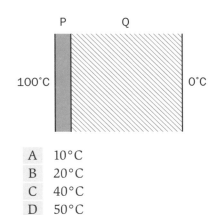

A   10°C
B   20°C
C   40°C
D   50°C
E   60°C

# Test 9

## 2

How many joules are required to heat 0.15 m³ of water from 10°C to 50°C for a hot bath if the specific heat capacity of water is 4200 J kg⁻¹ K⁻¹ and its density is 1000 kg m⁻³?

A   25.2 J
B   $11.2 \times 10^9$ J
C   $2.52 \times 10^6$ J
D   $2.52 \times 10^3$ kJ
E   25.2 MJ

## 3

An electric heater raises the temperature of 0.10 kg of water in a very thin vessel through 10°C in 2 minutes. When placed in 0.05 kg of water, how long does it take to raise the temperature by 15°C?

A   2 minutes.
B   15 minutes.
C   800 seconds.
D   9000 seconds.
E   90 seconds.

## 4

The occupant of a house wants to reduce fuel bills by changing the construction of a double-glazed window (i.e. a window which has a layer of air trapped between two parallel-sided pieces of glass). Bearing in mind that the thermal conductivity of glass is about 40 times that of air, the best way to do this would be to:

A   Halve the thickness of the glass panes.
B   Double the thickness of the glass panes.
C   Double the thickness of the air space.
D   Halve the thickness of the air space.
E   Halve the area of the window.

## 5

50 g of ice at 0°C is melted, heated to 100°C and then completely evaporated. If the specific latent heat of vaporisation is $2.3 \times 10^6$ J kg⁻¹, the specific latent heat of fusion is $3.2 \times 10^5$ J kg⁻¹ and the specific heat capacity of water is 4200 J kg⁻¹ K⁻¹, then the total amount of heat required will be:

A   $485 \times 10^5$ J
B   $1310 \times 10^5$ J
C   $1.31 \times 10^5$ J
D   $1.52 \times 10^5$ J
E   $152 \times 10^5$ J

QUESTION

**6**

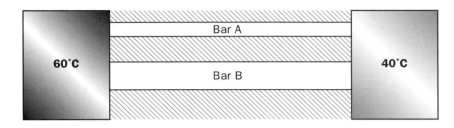

Bar A

60°C      40°C

Bar B

Two thermally conducting blocks are maintained at the temperatures shown.
Bar A and Bar B are both of length 40 cm and of the same material (thermal conductivity
25 W m$^{-1}$ K$^{-1}$).

Cross sectional area of bar A is $1.0 \times 10^{-4}$ m$^2$.
Cross sectional area of bar B is $4.0 \times 10^{-4}$ m$^2$.

The space between the blocks and the
bars is thermally insulated.

The total rate of heat flow (in W)
between the blocks is:

| | |
|---|---|
| A | 50 |
| B | 0.63 |
| C | 0.23 |
| D | 0.25 |
| E | 0.13 |

**7**

A bullet of lead (specific heat capacity
130 J kg$^{-1}$ K$^{-1}$) is fired with a speed of
250 m s$^{-1}$. If its original temperature is
300 K, the maximum temperature
(in K) it can reach on impact is:

| | |
|---|---|
| A | 540 |
| B | 240 |
| C | 301 |
| D | 961 |
| E | 1260 |

**8**

A brick wall is 50 times thicker than a
glass window and the thermal
conductivity of brick is about $^1/_6$ that
of glass. The temperature differences
across the wall and the window are
the same. If the rate of heat flow/unit
area through the brick is $p$ times that
through the glass, then $p$ is:

| | |
|---|---|
| A | 300 |
| B | 50/6 |
| C | 6/50 |
| D | 1/300 |
| E | $(6/50)^2$ |

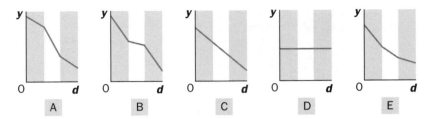

The cavity wall of a house is constructed using two layers of bricks separated by an equal thickness of air. The brick is a much better conductor of heat than the air. Steady state has been reached and the inner surface of the wall is warmest.

Which of the above graphs represents:

**9** Variation of temperature ($y$) with distance ($d$) from the inside wall.

**10** Rate of flow of heat ($y$) with distance ($d$) from the inside wall.

**Time allowed:** *1 hour 20 minutes*

## Section 1: Short Questions

**1**

Describe an experiment for demonstrating Brownian Motion in air.
Explain exactly how the observations support the theory that gas particles undergo random motion.

**2**

What do the symbols $n$ and $R$ represent in the equation $pV = nRT$?
A 100 W electric lamp is filled with argon to a pressure of $1.0 \times 10^5$ Pa when its temperature is 17°C. The molar mass of argon is 40 g and the value of $R$ is $8.3 \text{ J mol}^{-1} \text{K}^{-1}$. Write down an estimate for the volume of argon in the lamp.
The temperature of the argon in the lamp when it has been switched on for some time is 57°C. Calculate:

**(a)** the mass of argon in the lamp, and
**(b)** the pressure in the lamp when it has been switched on for some time.

**3**

**(a)** A flask is filled with water vapour at 30°C and sealed. The velocity of any particular water vapour molecule in the flask may vary randomly in two different ways. What are these two ways?
Describe, with the aid of a diagram, how the motion of one of the water vapour molecules could change during a time interval in which it has six collisions with other molecules.
**(b)** Explain why a small increase in pressure will do more work on a gas than on a liquid.

**4**

The kinetic theory explains the properties of a gas in terms of the motion of its particles.

**(a)** State four major assumptions of the theory.
**(b)** Use the kinetic theory to explain in detail how a gas exerts a pressure on the walls of a container.
**(c)** Why does the pressure increase when the temperature rises, assuming the volume of the container stays the same?

**5**

State the ideal gas equation.

(a) Explain the meaning of each symbol in the equation.
(b) The tyre on a bicycle contains 500 cm³ of air when the pressure is 150 kPa.
   If the temperature stays the same, what would the volume be if the pressure rose to 200 kPa?
(c) In practice the temperature does not stay the same. Why not?
(d) If the tyre bursts, the temperature tends to fall. Why?

**6**

State Boyle's Law for an ideal gas.
An experiment to demonstrate this law gave the following readings.

| $P$/kPa | 150 | 300 | 450 | 600 | 750 |
|---------|-----|-----|-----|-----|-----|
| $V$/cm³ | 200 | 102 | 66 | 50 | 40 |

Plot a graph and show clearly that it demonstrates that Boyle's Law is true.

**7**

Explain how you would conduct an experiment to show how the pressure of a gas at constant temperature varies with its density.

## Section 2: Multiple Choice

*Select one answer only for each question.*

**1**

At temperature $T$, the average speed of the molecules of an ideal gas is $c$. The temperature of the gas is changed by halving the pressure (at constant volume).
The average speed of the molecules is now:

  A   $c/\sqrt{2}$
  B   $c\sqrt{2}$
  C   $c/2$
  D   $c/4$
  E   $2c$

**2**

| 2 litres |
|----------|
| $10 \times 10^4$ Pa |

X        Y

| 6 litres |
|----------|
| $2 \times 10^4$ Pa |

Two containers at the same temperature are initially separate but can be connected by a narrow pipe containing a valve.

Initially container X contains two litres of an ideal gas at a pressure of $10 \times 10^4$ Pa. Container Y contains six litres of ideal gas at a pressure of $2 \times 10^4$ Pa.

When joined together the final equilibrium pressure will be:

A   $2.0 \times 10^4$ Pa
B   $4.0 \times 10^4$ Pa
C   $5.0 \times 10^4$ Pa
D   $8.0 \times 10^4$ Pa
E   $10.0 \times 10^4$ Pa

**QUESTION**

**3**

A group of particles have speeds $3\,\mathrm{m\,s^{-1}}$, $4\,\mathrm{m\,s^{-1}}$, $5\,\mathrm{m\,s^{-1}}$, $6\,\mathrm{m\,s^{-1}}$, $7\,\mathrm{m\,s^{-1}}$. The root mean square speed (in $\mathrm{m\,s^{-1}}$) is:

A   5.2
B   5.0
C   2.2
D   7.6
E   10.4

**4**

When the volume of a fixed mass of gas at constant temperature is doubled, the pressure is halved because:

A   Number of molecules is halved.
B   Average momentum of molecules is halved.
C   Average kinetic energy of molecules is halved.
D   Average velocity of molecules is halved.
E   Number of collisions made by the molecules per second per unit area of the wall is halved.

**5**

A

16 atmospheres

8 litres

$4 \times 10^{23}$ molecules

B

8 atmospheres

4 litres

$8 \times 10^{23}$ molecules

Two vessels contain gases as shown above.

The ratio $\dfrac{\text{temperature of gas in A}}{\text{temperature of gas in B}}$ is:

A   $1/8$
B   8
C   $1/4$
D   4
E   1

**6**

A cylinder of 8 litre capacity contains gas N at a pressure of 24 kPa. Another cylinder, 4 litre capacity, contains gas M at a pressure of 12 kPa. These gases do not react together chemically. When the two cylinders are connected together the resulting pressure (in kPa) will be:

A   20
B   22
C   24
D   26
E   28

**7**

The RMS speed of an oxygen molecule varies with temperature. At 300 K the RMS speed is $c$. At what temperature (in K) is the RMS speed $2c$?

A   2292
B   1200
C   1146
D   600
E   425

**8**

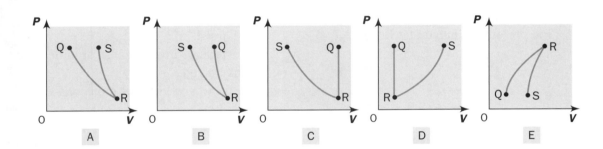

A fixed mass of gas is at pressure $P_1$ at Q. It is expanded reversibly and isothermally to R and then compressed reversibly and adiabatically to S, where the pressure is again $P_1$. Which of the above graphs represents these changes?

**9**

In an experiment to demonstrate Brownian motion in a gas, the observer sees large numbers of bright specks of light moving jerkily in random directions.

Which of the following statements is correct?

A   The motion of the gas molecules is being observed.
B   The bright specks move faster if the temperature of the gas is raised.
C   The gas molecules are scattering the light.
D   If the pressure of the gas is raised the specks change direction less frequently.
E   The movement of the light specks is due to an interchange of potential energy.

**QUESTION**

**10**

The molar heat capacity of an ideal gas at constant pressure is larger than that at constant volume because:

A  The molecules move faster as the gas expands.

B  The force of attraction of the molecules decreases when the gas expands.

C  The molecules occupy less space when the gas expands.

D  Work is done against external pressure as the gas expands.

E  Work is done against the intermolecular forces as the gas expands.

# Test 11

## Current electricity

**Time allowed:** *1 hour 20 minutes*

# Section 1: Short Questions

**QUESTION**

**1**

**(a)** Sketch and label a graph to show how you would expect the current in a 12 V, 24 W tungsten filament lamp to change as the potential difference across the lamp increases slowly from 0 V to 12 V.

**(b)** Describe briefly how you would check your graph experimentally.

**(c)** Explain whether or not you think the filament obeys Ohm's Law.

**2**

Show how the equation $I = nAve$ follows from the meanings attached to the symbols. Explain why the resistivity of an intrinsic semiconductor decreases as its temperature rises.

**3**

The diagram shows a cell of e.m.f. $E$ and internal resistance $r$ connected in series with a variable resistor R. The current, $I$, in the resistor is measured with an ammeter and the potential difference, $V$, between its ends is measured with a voltmeter.

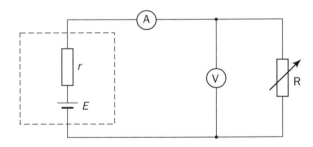

$E$, $I$, $V$ and $r$ are related as follows:

$V = E - Ir$

You are asked to use this circuit to find the values of $E$ and $r$ from a graph.

**(a)** State what measurements you would make.

**(b)** What graph would you plot? Sketch the graph you would expect to obtain and label the axes clearly.

**(c)** How would you use the graph to find $E$ and $r$?

**QUESTION**

**4**

(a) The diagram shows an a.c. power source E in series with a diode and a resistor. The potential difference between A and B is applied to the Y-input of an oscilloscope. Assuming a suitable setting for the time base controlling the X-deflection, sketch diagrams that show the pattern of the trace seen on the oscilloscope:

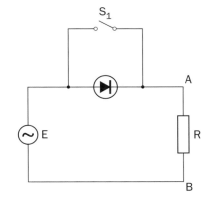

    (i)  with $S_1$ closed;
    (ii)  with $S_1$ open.

(b) What is the principal difference between alternating current and direct current?
(c) Calculate the peak current in a 60 W lamp working from a 240 V (rms) supply.

**5**

The light-dependent resistor (LDR) in the circuit on the right is found to have resistance 800 Ω in moonlight and resistance 160 Ω in daylight. Calculate the voltmeter reading $V_m$ in moonlight with the switch S open.

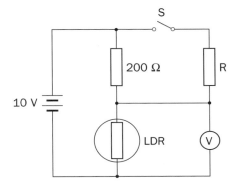

If the reading of the voltmeter in daylight with the switch S closed is also equal to $V_m$, what is the value of the resistance $R$?

**6**

(a) Define electrical resistance.
(b) The graph represents a current–voltage characteristic for an ohmic conductor. Use the graph to find its electrical resistance.
(c) Give an example of a non-ohmic conductor and sketch its characteristic.

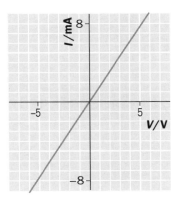

**7**

Describe in detail an experiment you could do in the laboratory to measure the resistivity of a piece of nichrome wire. You should include:

(a) A circuit diagram.
(b) A list of measurements to be made.
(c) Formulae to show the calculation.

## Section 2: Multiple Choice

*Select one answer only for each question.*

QUESTION

**1**

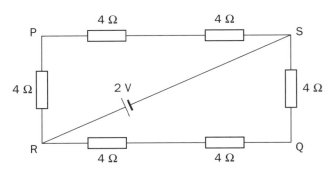

In the above circuit the potential difference (in V) across PQ is:

A   8/9
B   8/3
C   2
D   4/3
E   2/3

**2**

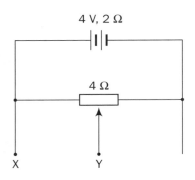

In the above circuit Y slides along the 4 Ω rheostat. The potential difference across XY varies (in V) from zero to:

A   4
B   1
C   2
D   $^{3}/_{8}$
E   $^{1}/_{2}$

**3**

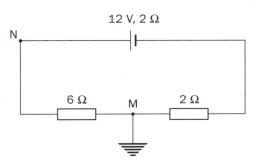

In the above circuit the battery has an e.m.f. of 12 V and an internal resistance of 2 Ω.

The point M is earthed. The potential (in V) at point N is:

A 12.0
B 10.0
C 8.0
D 7.2
E 2.4

QUESTION 4

A heater rated at 36 W is to be operated from a 12 V supply and made of wire of resistivity $2.5 \times 10^{-7}$ m. If the only wire available has a cross-sectional area of 0.5 mm² then the length required will be:

A 0.8 m
B 8.0 m
C 80 cm
D 80 m
E 800 m

**5**

A moving coil meter of resistance 25 Ω has a full scale deflection of 4.0 mA. It could be converted to a milliammeter with full scale deflection of 50 mA by adding a resistance (in Ω) of:

A 1.25 (in series)
B 2.17 (in series)
C 2.17 (in parallel)
D 1.25 (in parallel)
E 1225 (in series)

**6–7**

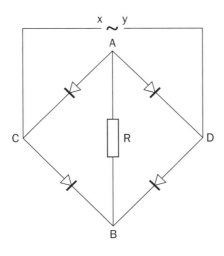

A circuit is set up as shown using an alternating supply and a bridge circuit with four diodes. Here are examples of five different waveforms.

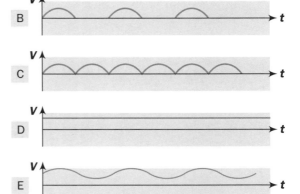

**6**

Which of these represents the potential difference across AB?

**7**

Which of these represents the potential difference across CD?

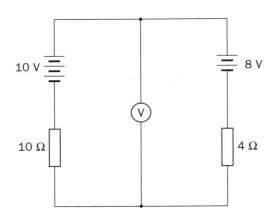

The cells in the above circuit have negligible internal resistance, but the voltmeter has a very high resistance. What is the reading (in V) on the voltmeter?

A   10.0

B   8.6

C   2.0

D   1.4

E   4.9

**9**

For two wires P and Q of different materials, their respective resistivities are in the ratio 1:2. Their respective diameters are in the ratio 1:2. Their respective lengths are in the ratio 1:2. The ratio of their resistances is:

A   16:1

B   8:1

C   4:1

D   2:1

E   1:1

**10**

A lamp is rated 12 V, 24 W. It is connected to a 10 V supply. The current (A) flowing will be approximately:

A   2.0

B   1.7

C   0.5

D   0.2

E   0.1

# Test 12

## Magnetic effects of electricity

**Time allowed:** *1 hour 20 minutes*

## Section 1: Short Questions

**QUESTION**

**1**

The force per unit length between two long parallel wires distance $r$ apart and carrying currents $I_1$ and $I_2$ is:

$$F = \frac{\mu_0 I_1 I_2}{2\pi r}$$

Sketch the form of a graph of $F$ against $r$ if $I_1$ and $I_2$ are fixed whilst $r$ is varied. What quantities would you plot in order to obtain a straight line? From this graph, how would you determine a value of the constant $\mu_0$, given the values of $I_1$ and $I_2$?

**2**

**(a)** Draw a diagram showing two parallel wires in which the currents are flowing in opposite directions. Show on the diagram:
   (i)   The direction of the resultant B-field at a point midway between the wires (ignoring the Earth's magnetic field).
   (ii)  The direction of the electromagnetic force on each wire.

**(b)** The ampère is defined as 'the constant current which, flowing in two infinitely long, straight parallel conductors of negligible circular cross-section, placed in a vacuum 1 m apart, produces between them a force per unit length of $2 \times 10^{-7}$ N m$^{-1}$.'

Using this definition and the equation given below for the force per unit length between two long and parallel conductors, deduce a value for $\mu_0$ and for the units in which it is measured.

$$\frac{F}{L} = \frac{\mu_0 I_1 I_2}{2\pi r}$$

**3**

The diagram shows two coils, each with $N$ turns. $N$ is a large number. The coils are threaded over a straight hollow plastic tube.
Coil A is connected to an a.c. supply and coil B is connected to a lamp. The lamp glows faintly.

**(a)** Trace the stages by which energy is transmitted from the a.c. supply to the lamp.

**(b)** Explain why the lamp brightens when an iron bar is put into the tube.

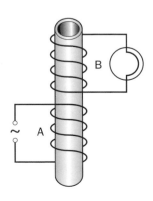

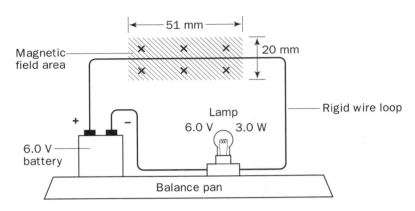

The diagram shows a rigid conducting wire loop connected to a 6 V battery through a 6.0 V, 3.0 W lamp. The circuit is standing on a top-pan balance. A uniform horizontal magnetic field of strength 50 mT acts at right angles to the straight top part of the conducting wire in the direction indicated in the diagram, i.e. into the paper. This magnetic field extends over the shaded area in the diagram. The balance reads 153.860 g. Calculate:

(a) The force exerted on the conducting wire by the magnetic field.

(b) The new balance reading if the direction of the magnetic field is reversed.

**5**

Sketch a diagram to show the magnetic field pattern around a long straight wire which is carrying a current of 1000 A.

Show:

(a) The direction of the current.

(b) The direction of the magnetic field.

(c) The strength of the magnetic flux density at a distance of 20 cm from the centre of the wire.

**6**

(a) State the laws of electromagnetic induction.

(b) Use the laws to explain why an e.m.f. is induced between the ends of the coil AB as the magnet falls.

(c) Sketch a graph to show how the e.m.f. would vary with time if the short bar magnet was dropped from above the coil to a point far below it.

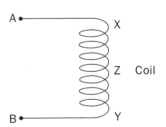

**7**

Define the tesla.

A solenoid is 50 cm long, has an area of cross-section of 1.0 cm$^2$ and has 1000 turns. It is connected in series with a cell of e.m.f. 1.5 V and internal resistance 0.2 $\Omega$. The resistance of the solenoid is 0.4 $\Omega$.

Calculate:

(a) The magnetic flux density at the centre of the solenoid.

(b) The total magnetic flux passing through the inside of the solenoid.

## Section 2: Multiple Choice

*Select one answer only for each question.*

**QUESTION 1**

A train is travelling due north with a speed of 15 m s$^{-1}$. A wheel axle under the front of the train cuts the vertical component of the earth's field ($4 \times 10^{-5}$ T). If the axle is 1.4 m long then the e.m.f. generated (in V) between the ends of the axle is:

A  $8.4 \times 10^{-4}$
B  $8.4 \times 10^{-5}$
C  $8.4 \times 10^{-6}$
D  $4.2 \times 10^{-4}$
E  $4.2 \times 10^{-5}$

**2**

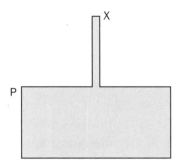 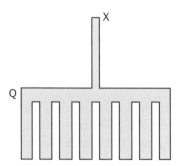

P and Q are two identical metal pendulums, except that P is solid and Q has slits cut in it. The pendulums are set swinging between the poles of a strong horseshoe magnet. Which of the following statements is true?

A  An e.m.f. is induced in P but not in Q.
B  An e.m.f. is induced in Q but not in P.
C  The pendulums are not affected by the magnetic field.
D  Q slows down first.
E  P slows down first.

**3**

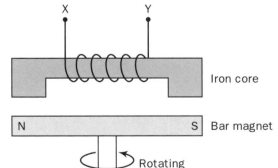

In the diagram above a bar magnet is rotating close to an iron core. A coil of wire is wound round the iron core. The e.m.f. produced between XY will be increased by:

A  Increasing the air gap between the core and the magnet.
B  Decreasing the number of turns on the coil.
C  Decreasing the diameter of the iron core.
D  Using a laminated core instead of a solid one.
E  Decreasing rate of rotation of the bar magnet.

QUESTION

4

What is the force/unit length (in $N\,m^{-1}$) on each of two long, straight, parallel wires placed 20 cm apart in air if currents of 2.0 A and 1.5 A flow in opposite directions in the wires? ($\mu_0 = 4\pi \times 10^{-7}\,H\,m^{-1}$)

| A | $3.0 \times 10^{-6}$ |
|---|---|
| B | $1.5 \times 10^{-6}$ |
| C | $3.0 \times 10^{-5}$ |
| D | $1.5 \times 10^{-5}$ |
| E | $3.0 \times 10^{-8}$ |

5

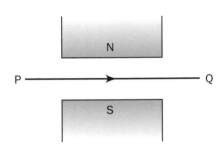

A wire carries a steady current from P to Q between the poles of a strong magnet. The resultant force on the wire is:

| A | Zero. |
|---|---|
| B | In the direction PQ. |
| C | In the direction NS. |
| D | In a direction perpendicular to PQ and NS. |
| E | Used to form a couple tending to rotate the wire. |

6

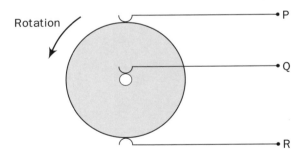

A metal disc is rotating with angular velocity $w$ in a uniform magnetic field directed perpendicular to the plane of the disc. Which of the following statements is incorrect? The e.m.f. induced across PQ is:

| A | The same magnitude as the e.m.f. induced across QR. |
|---|---|
| B | Increased by increasing the speed of rotation. |
| C | Increased by increasing the strength of the magnetic field. |
| D | Increased by increasing the radius of the disc. |
| E | Equal to the e.m.f. induced across PR. |

**QUESTION**

**7**

Two long, straight, parallel, vertical wires P and Q carry currents of 2 A and 5 A, respectively. The force per unit length acting on P is $2 \times 10^{-5}$ N to the right.
The force per unit length acting on Q is:

A   $5 \times 10^{-5}$ N to the left.
B   $5 \times 10^{-5}$ N to the right.
C   $2 \times 10^{-5}$ N to the left.
D   $2 \times 10^{-5}$ N to the right.
E   $3 \times 10^{-5}$ N to the left.

**8**

A long, vertical, straight wire carries a steady current $I$ in a location where there is also a uniform horizontal magnetic flux of $2.0 \times 10^{-5}$ T. If zero resultant flux density is found at a point 15 cm from the wire, then the current in the wire (taking $\mu_0 = 4\pi \times 10^{-7}$ H m$^{-1}$) in ampères is approximately:

A   0
B   15.0
C   30.0
D   7.5
E   4.8

**9**

An air cored solenoid carries a current of 2.0 A. It is 50.0 cm long and has 400 turns. What is the magnetic flux density (in T) at its centre?
($\mu_0 = 4\pi \times 10^{-7}$ H m$^{-1}$)

A   $64.0 \times 10^{-5}$
B   $5.0 \times 10^{-4}$
C   $2.0 \times 10^{-5}$
D   $1.0 \times 10^{-3}$
E   $2.0 \times 10^{-3}$

**10**

A simple a.c. generator consists of a coil rotating in a steady magnetic field. The amplitude of the induced e.m.f. could be increased by:

A   Reducing the resistance of the coil.
B   Increasing the resistance of the coil.
C   Decreasing the number of turns in the coil.
D   Increasing the speed of rotation of the coil.
E   Decreasing the cross-sectional area of the coil.

# est 13

# Electric and gravitational fields

**Time allowed:** *1 hour 20 minutes*

## Section 1: Short Questions

**QUESTION**

**1**

What do you understand by:

**(a)** A gravitational field?
**(b)** Gravitational field strength?

A satellite is circling a planet of mass $M$ in a circular orbit of radius $r$. If $T$ is the time period of the satellite, show that $T^2 = 4\pi^2 r^3/GM$.

**2**

**(a)** Define $G$.
**(b)** What is the difference between $G$ and $g$?
**(c)** Give an outline of the historical experiment that was performed to find a value for $G$. (Your description should give the physics principles involved.)

**3**

State Newton's Universal Law of Gravitation.

A research satellite, mass 100 kg, is in a circular orbit around the earth. It is approximately $1.0 \times 10^6$ km from the earth's centre. Calculate:

**(a)** Weight of the satellite in this orbit.
**(b)** An approximate value for the decrease in gravitational potential energy when the distance of the satellite from the earth's centre goes down by 1.0 km.
**(c)** Why is the answer in **(b)** an approximation?

(Take $G = 6.7 \times 10^6 \, \text{N m}^2 \, \text{kg}^{-2}$ and mass of earth $= 6.0 \times 10^{24}$ kg.)

**4**

Define electric field strength at a point.

Draw a diagram to illustrate:

**(a)** Electric field around a point charge.
**(b)** Electric field between two parallel plates with a p.d. across them.

**QUESTION**

**5**

A force $F$ can vary with distance $r$ from a fixed point according to $F = kr^{-2}$ where $k$ is a constant. Sketch graphs of:

(a) $F$ against $r$;
(b) $F$ against $1/r^2$.

State two situations in which this equation could apply.

**6**

The moon rotates around the earth.
(a) What is the time period of the moon?
(b) Draw a free body diagram for the moon.
(c) State Newton's Third Law.
(d) Explain how Newton's Third Law applies to the moon rotating round the earth.

**7**

(a) Two positive charges are situated 1 cm apart in air. The charge on each is $2.0 \times 10^{-9}$ C. If the force was $1.0 \times 10^{-5}$, what would the distance be?
(b) An electron starting with zero velocity is accelerated through a p.d. of 600 V. What velocity does the electron acquire?
You may like to know:  $\varepsilon_0 = 8.85 \times 10^{-12}$ F m$^{-1}$
$$e = 1.6 \times 10^{-19} \text{ C}$$
$$m_e = 9.0 \times 10^{-31} \text{ kg.}$$

## Section 2: Multiple Choice

*Select one answer only for each question.*

**1**

Which of the following statements about alpha particles is incorrect?

A  They are deflected by magnetic fields.
B  They are deflected by electric fields.
C  They are helium nuclei.
D  They contain two protons and two neutrons.
E  They can pass through a thin sheet of metal.

**2**

The mass of the earth is about $6 \times 10^{24}$ kg and the mass of the sun is about $2 \times 10^{30}$ kg. Compared with the force exerted by the sun on the earth, the force exerted by the earth on the sun is:

A  Much less.
B  A little less.
C  The same.
D  A little more.
E  Much more.

**3**

If a stationary electron is subjected to a uniform electric field its resultant motion will be:

A  Unchanged.
B  Motion in a circular path.
C  Motion in a parabolic path.
D  Motion in a straight line.
E  Oscillation about a fixed point.

· · · · · · · · · · · · · · · · · · · · · · · · · · · · · · · · · · · · ·

**4**

Two point charges $q_1$ and $q_2$ are placed a distance $x$ apart in air. The force between $q_1$ and $q_2$ can be halved by:

A  Doubling distance $x$.
B  Halving both $q_1$ and $q_2$.
C  Doubling both $q_1$ and $q_2$.
D  Halving distance $x$.
E  Halving either $q_1$ or $q_2$.

· · · · · · · · · · · · · · · · · · · · · · · · · · · · · · · · · · · · ·

**5**

Two identical spheres are in contact with one another. Each sphere has mass $m$ and radius $r$. If the gravitational attraction between them is $F$, what will the gravitational attraction be if one sphere is moved away through a distance of $2r$?

A  $^1/_4F$
B  $^1/_9F$
C  $4F$
D  $9F$
E  $^1/_2F$

· · · · · · · · · · · · · · · · · · · · · · · · · · · · · · · · · · · · ·

**6**

The force between two point charges $Q_1$ and $Q_2$ placed distance $r$ apart in a vacuum is directly proportional to:

A  $(Q_1 + Q_2)/r^2$
B  $Q_1\,Q_2/r^2$
C  $Q_1\,Q_2r^2$
D  $(Q_1 + Q_2)/r$
E  $Q_1\,Q_2/r$

· · · · · · · · · · · · · · · · · · · · · · · · · · · · · · · · · · · · ·

**7**

A mass of 100 kg is situated on a planet where the gravitational field strength is 5 N $kg^{-1}$. What is the gravitational force (in N) on the mass?

A  500
B  25
C  50
D  250
E  5

· · · · · · · · · · · · · · · · · · · · · · · · · · · · · · · · · · · · ·

# Test 13

**QUESTION**

**8**

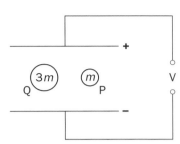

An electric field acts on two charged spheres as shown in the diagram. Particle P has mass $m$. Particle Q has mass $3m$. They are both stationary. If the plates are moved further apart:

A  P accelerates up at a rate that is greater than Q.

B  P accelerates down at a rate that is greater than Q.

C  P and Q both remain stationary.

D  P and Q both begin to move up with the same acceleration.

E  P and Q both begin to move down with the same acceleration.

**9**

A satellite is in orbit very slightly above the surface of a planet. The time period of the satellite is $T$. The density of the planet is $\Delta$. The quantity $T^2\Delta$ is approximately equal to:

A  $3\pi G$

B  $4\pi^2 G$

C  $1/G$

D  $3\pi/G$

E  $4\pi^2/G$

**10**

If $x$ represents the electric field intensity between two parallel plates and $y$ represents the distance between the plates, which of the following is correct?

A  $\ln(x) = k\ln(y)$

B  $x = ky^{-1}$

C  $x = ky^{-2}$

D  $x = ky$

E  $x = ky^2$

# Test 14
## Capacitors

**Time allowed:** *1 hour 20 minutes*

## Section 1: Short Questions

QUESTION

1

A capacitor is connected to a d.c. supply through a resistor. The graph below shows how the charge on the capacitor increases with time.

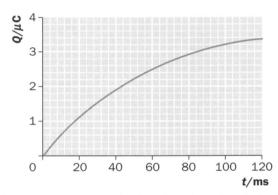

Calculate a value for the average current in the charging circuit during the interval $t = 40$ ms to $t = 100$ ms.
Find the instantaneous value for the current at time $t = 40$ ms.
With reference to these two results, explain how instantaneous current is described as 'the limiting value of an average current'.

2

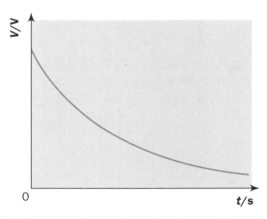

A 3 $\mu$F capacitor is first fully charged and then discharges through a 0.4 M$\Omega$ resistor. The graph above shows how the potential difference, $V$, across the resistor changes with time. Calculate the time constant for this circuit.

How long will it take for $V$ to drop from 8.00 V to 2.94 V?
How would the graph differ if the resistance had been 2 M$\Omega$?
Explain, in atomic terms, what happens in the circuit during the discharge process.
Describe clearly in these terms the effect of increasing the resistance.

A capacitor consists of two parallel metal plates in air. The distance between the plates is 5.00 mm and the capacitance is 72 pF. The potential difference between the plates is raised to 12.0 V with a battery.

(a) Calculate the energy stored in the capacitor.
(b) The battery is then disconnected from the capacitor; the capacitor retains its charge. Calculate the energy stored in the capacitor if the distance between the plates is now increased to 10.00 mm.

The answers to (a) and (b) are different. Why is this so?

Use your answers to estimate the average force of attraction between the plates while the separation is being increased.

**4**

A 9.0 V battery is connected in series with a 2000 $\mu$F capacitor. The capacitor, fully charged, is now disconnected from the battery and discharged through a 200 k$\Omega$ resistor.

(a) Find the time constant for the circuit.
(b) Draw a labelled circuit diagram of the arrangement.
(c) State clearly the measurements you would make to enable you to draw a graph showing how the p.d. across the capacitor varies with time during the discharge.

**5**

(a) Derive a formula for the energy stored in a charged capacitor.
(b) Calculate the energy stored in a 3.0 $\mu$F capacitor charged from a 20 V battery.
(c) This charged capacitor is connected in series with a 10.0 M$\Omega$ resistor and an uncharged identical 3.0 $\mu$F capacitor. Calculate the energy dissipated in the 10.0 M$\Omega$ resistor.
(d) What effect does the resistor have on the process?

**6**

(a) Define capacitance.
(b) A capacitor consisting of two parallel metal plates is connected in series with a switch and a battery. Explain what happens to the distribution of charge in the circuit when the switch is closed.
(c) What difference would it make if the battery was replaced by an alternating source?

**7**

Describe experiments you could perform to test how the capacitance of a parallel plate capacitor is affected by:

(a) The area of the plates.
(b) The separation of the plates.

## Section 2: Multiple Choice

*Select one answer only for each question.*

QUESTION

**1**

When two identical capacitors are connected in series the total capacitance is 2 $\mu$F. When connected in parallel the total capacitance (in $\mu$F) is:

A   16
B   8
C   4
D   2
E   1

**2**

The following graphs show how one physical quantity ($y$) varies with another physical quantity ($x$)

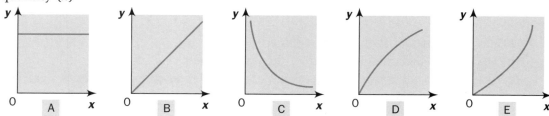

Which graph approximates closest to the relationship between these variables?

$y$ axis – electric charges stored on a parallel plate capacitor when a battery is connected across its plates.
$x$ axis – distance between the plates.

**3**

A capacitor of 9.0 $\mu$F is charged from a 200 V source. The capacitor is disconnected and placed in parallel with a capacitor of 3.0 $\mu$F. What is the potential difference (in V) across the two capacitors?

A   17
B   33
C   100
D   150
E   200

**4**

Three 1.00 $\mu$F capacitors are connected in series with a 2.00 V battery. The charge on each capacitor is:

A   2 $\mu$C
B   2 × 10$^{-3}$ C
C   2 C
D   2/3 $\mu$C
E   2/3 mC

**QUESTION**

**5**

A capacitor of $6 \times 10^{-4}$ $\mu$F is charged 100 times every second using a 10 V supply and then discharged at the same rate through a microammeter. The current in microamps will be:

A  0.6
B  6.0
C  $6.0 \times 10^{-3}$
D  $1.7 \times 10^{-3}$
E  1.7

**6**

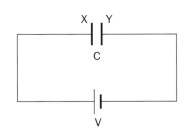

A capacitor and a battery are connected as shown.
If plate Y is moved further away from X which of these statements is incorrect?

A  Energy stored by the capacitor increases.
B  Capacitance decreases.
C  Potential difference across the plates stays the same.
D  Charge on the plates decreases.
E  Energy is taken from the battery.

**7**

Two identical parallel plate capacitors $C_1$ and $C_2$ are connected as shown in the diagram.

To decrease the capacitance between X and Y:

A  Connect $C_1$ and $C_2$ in parallel.
B  Place an insulating material between the plates of both capacitors.
C  Double the plate separation of one capacitor.
D  Halve the plate separation of both capacitors.
E  Short out one capacitor.

**8**

A capacitor with air between its plates is connected to a 1.5 V battery. The space between the plates is then filled with a dielectric of relative permittivity 2.0. Which of these is not changed?

A  p.d. across the plates.
B  Capacitance of the capacitor.
C  Energy stored in the capacitor.
D  Charge on the positive plate.
E  Charge on the negative plate.

Four identical capacitors are connected in different ways.
Which arrangement gives the largest capacitance?

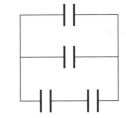

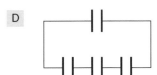

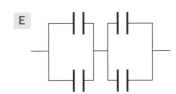

10

A capacitor of 8.0 $\mu$F is charged by connecting it to a 200 V supply. Another capacitor of 4.0 $\mu$F is charged by connecting it to an 800 V supply. They are then connected together so that similarly charged plates are joined. The new p.d. (in V) across the combination will be:

| | |
|---|---|
| A | 400 |
| B | 800 |
| C | 1000 |
| D | 133 |
| E | 300 |

**Time allowed:** *1 hour 20 minutes*

## Section 1: Short Questions

QUESTION

**1**

$^{226}_{88}$Ra decays into $^{222}_{86}$Rn with a half-life of $1.6 \times 10^3$ years.

**(a)** Write down the nuclear reaction that describes the decay.
**(b)** Describe a simple experiment, using a Geiger counter with a thin end window, which would support your answer to **(a)**.
**(c)** What fraction of a sample of $^{226}_{88}$Ra decays in $1.0 \times 10^3$ years?

**2**

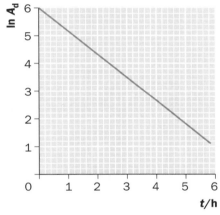

Explain what is meant by the half-life of a radioactive nuclide. Write down the relationship between the half-life and the decay constant. The graph shows how ln $A_d$ (where $A_d$ is the activity per minute) changes with time, $t$, during the decay of a radioactive nuclide. Use the graph to find:

**(a)** The initial activity.
**(b)** The decay constant for the nuclide.

**3**

Living matter contains carbon. A tiny proportion of this carbon is the radioactive isotope $^{14}$C. The average decay rate of the $^{14}$C content per kilogram of carbon in living matter is 255 Bq (i.e. 255 disintegrations per second). The half-life of $^{14}$C is $1.76 \times 10^{11}$ s.

**(a)** Calculate:
    (i) The decay constant for $^{14}$C;
    (ii) The probable number of $^{14}$C atoms per kilogram of carbon in living matter.
**(b)** Explain, with reference to the average decay rate of 255 Bq, why radioactivity is described as a random phenomenon.

**4**

A specimen contains $N$ atoms. The decay rate $dN/dt$ is given by $dN/dt = -\lambda N$, where $\lambda$ is the decay constant. The decay constant for radon is $12.6 \times 10^{-3}$ s$^{-1}$ and at a particular time the decay rate is $6.4 \times 10^3$ Bq.

Calculate the number of radon atoms present at this time.

**5**

In a process called fusion, nuclei combine at high temperatures. An example of such a reaction would be:

$$^2_1\text{H} + {}^3_1\text{H} = {}^1_0\text{n} + {}^4_2\text{He}$$

**(a)** Explain the meaning of 'isotope' in this example.

**(b)** How do you know that charge is conserved?

**(c)** How do you know the number of nucleons remains constant?

**(d)** Is mass conserved?

**6**

Explain the meaning of the term 'radioactive' material.

What do these terms mean?

**(a)** $\alpha$ particle;

**(b)** $\beta$ particle;

**(c)** $\gamma$ particle.

**7**

Describe an experiment that you could do in the laboratory to find the half-life of a radioactive gas.

## Section 2: Multiple Choice

*Select one answer only for each question.*

**1**

The radioactive nucleus of $^{214}_{82}\text{Pb}$ decays with the emission of $\beta$ and $\gamma$. The resultant nucleus will contain:

A   83 protons and 131 neutrons.

B   81 protons and 133 neutrons.

C   83 protons and 214 neutrons.

D   81 protons and 214 neutrons.

E   78 protons and 134 neutrons.

**2**

When a radium nucleus $^{226}_{88}\text{Ra}$ decays, the mass of the products is less than the mass of the original atom.

The mass defect is $8.8 \times 10^{-30}$ kg.

If Planck's constant $h = 6.6 \times 10^{-34}$ J s and speed of light in vacuo $c = 3.0 \times 10^8$ m s$^{-1}$, the energy released, in joules, is:

A   $7.92 \times 10^{-15}$

B   $7.92 \times 10^{-13}$

C   $7.92 \times 10^{-21}$

D   $2.64 \times 10^{-21}$

E   $2.64 \times 10^{-20}$

**3**

A radioactive sample contains $74 \times 10^{10}$ atoms originally. If its half-life is 10 hours, how many atoms will be left not disintegrated after 15 hours?

A  $32 \times 10^{10}$
B  $49 \times 10^{11}$
C  $49 \times 10^{10}$
D  $26 \times 10^{11}$
E  $26 \times 10^{10}$

**4**

The number of atoms $N$ of a particular sample decays to one half of the original in 20 days. How much of the original will be left after 100 days?

A  $N/5$
B  $N/10$
C  $N/8$
D  $N/16$
E  $N/32$

**5**

The following equation represents a nuclear reaction
$$^{1}_{1}H + {}^{13}_{6}C \rightarrow {}^{14}_{7}N$$
If atomic mass of $^{1}_{1}H$ + atomic mass of $^{13}_{6}C$ = 14.011179 u and atomic mass of $^{14}_{7}N$ = 14.003074 u, it can be deduced that this reaction:

A  Cannot take place.
B  Will result in the emission of energy.
C  Involves the emission of a charged particle.
D  Involves the emission of an uncharged particle.
E  Means energy must be absorbed.

**6**

If the decay constant of a radioactive nuclide is $2.5 \times 10^{-7}$ s$^{-1}$ what is its half-life (in s)?

A  $2.8 \times 10^{6}$
B  $2.8 \times 10^{-6}$
C  $4.0 \times 10^{6}$
D  $4.0 \times 10^{-6}$
E  $2.5 \times 10^{-7}$

**7**

The count rate of a radioactive material goes down from 2048 counts per minute to 256 counts per minute in 3 min. After 4 min the count rate will be:

A  512
B  82
C  107
D  128
E  64

**8**

The rate of decay d$N$/d$t$ of the number $N$ of nuclei present in a sample of a radioactive nuclide at time $t$ is:

A  Proportional to $N$.
B  Proportional to $t$.
C  Proportional to $1/t$.
D  Proportional to $1/N$.
E  Equal to decay constant.

9

All the isotopes of a given nuclide must have exactly the same:

| A | Emissions from nucleus. |
| B | Half-life. |
| C | Number of neutrons in nucleus. |
| D | Number of protons in nucleus. |
| E | Number of nucleons in nucleus. |

10

Radioactive decay results in changes in nucleon and proton number of the original nuclide. If the decay results in an isotope of the original nucleus, then the following emission has occurred:

| A | $\alpha + \alpha + \alpha + \alpha + \beta$ |
| B | $\alpha + \beta$ |
| C | $\alpha + \alpha + \beta$ |
| D | $\alpha + \beta + \beta$ |
| E | $\alpha + \beta + \beta + \beta + \beta$ |

# Test 16

## Atomic processes

**Time allowed:** *1 hour 20 minutes*

## Section 1: Short Questions

**QUESTION 1**

A beam of electrons travelling with speed $1.2 \times 10^7$ m s$^{-1}$ in an evacuated tube is made to move in a circular path of radius 0.048 m by a uniform magnetic field of flux density $B = 1.4$ mT.

**(a)** Calculate, in electronvolts, the kinetic energy of an electron in the beam.
(The charge on an electron $= 1.6 \times 10^{-19}$ C and 1 eV $= 1.6 \times 10^{-19}$ J.)

**(b)** A similar technique is used to accelerate protons to very high speeds. Protons with energies of 500 GeV can be held by magnetic fields in circular orbits of radius 2 km. Suggest why such a large radius orbit is necessary for high energy protons.

**2**

The ionisation energy for hydrogen is 13.6 eV and the first and second excitation energies are 10.2 eV and 12.1 eV, respectively.

Draw an energy level diagram showing the ground state and the next two energy levels for hydrogen. Mark on the diagram the values of the energies corresponding to each level.

Mark on your diagram the transition between two of these levels that would result in the emission of radiation of the longest wavelength. Calculate the value of this wavelength.

1 eV $= 1.6 \times 10^{-19}$ J
Planck's constant $= 6.6 \times 10^{-34}$ J s
Speed of light $= 3.0 \times 10^8$ m s$^{-1}$.

**3**

The smallest quantity of energy that can be emitted from a source of gamma radiation of a particular frequency is $2 \times 10^{-11}$ J, but the smallest quantity of energy which can be emitted from a source of radio waves of a particular frequency is $6 \times 10^{-28}$ J. Explain why this is so.

QUESTION

4

A hydrogen atom emits light of wavelength 121.5 nm and 102.5 nm when it returns to its ground state from its first and second excited states respectively.
Calculate:
(a) The corresponding photon energies.
(b) The wavelength of light emitted when the atom passes from the second excited state to the first.

Speed of light, $c = 3.00 \times 10^8$ m s$^{-1}$
Planck's constant, $h = 6.63 \times 10^{-34}$ J s.

**5**

Describe the $\alpha$ scattering experiment devised by Rutherford to gain information on the structure of the nucleus.
What were the main conclusions from this experiment?

**6**

(a) Explain what is meant by the photoelectric effect. You should particularly include the meaning of the following terms: threshold wavelength and work function.
(b) A metal surface is illuminated with visible light of wavelength $5.0 \times 10^{-7}$ m. Photo-electrons are emitted with maximum energy $2.4 \times 10^{-19}$ J. Calculate the work function of the surface.
(c) When ultraviolet light is used on the same surface, electrons are also emitted, but this time their maximum energy is $9.0 \times 10^{-19}$ J. What is the wavelength of the ultraviolet light?

Planck's constant $= 6.6 \times 10^{-34}$ J s
Speed of light in a vacuum $= 3.00 \times 10^8$ m s$^{-1}$.

**7**

Describe an experiment which allows you to estimate the diameter of an oil molecule.
You should include:

(a) A labelled diagram.
(b) A list of measurements.
(c) Detail of the calculation.
(d) Any assumptions made.

## Section 2: Multiple Choice

*Select one answer only for each question.*

**1**

Which of the following has the same units as Planck's constant?

| A | Force × time × distance. |
| B | Force × time × (distance)$^{-1}$. |
| C | Energy × (time)$^{-1}$. |
| D | Mass × acceleration × time. |
| E | Power × time. |

**QUESTION**

**2**

In an experiment to demonstrate the photoelectric effect it was found that electrons were only emitted if the wavelength of the incident light was less than $7.0 \times 10^{-7}$ m. The minimum energy (in J) required to release electrons from the surface being used is:

$h = 6.6 \times 10^{-34}$ J s
$c = 3.0 \times 10^{8}$ m s$^{-1}$

A   $2.8 \times 10^{-19}$
B   $1.4 \times 10^{-19}$
C   $7.0 \times 10^{-7}$
D   $14.0 \times 10^{-7}$
E   $28.0 \times 10^{-7}$

**3**

When ultraviolet light falls on a metal surface, electrons are emitted. The rate of emission depends on the:

A   Temperature of the metal.
B   Electric potential of the metal.
C   Work function of the metal.
D   Wavelength of the radiation.
E   Intensity of the radiation.

**4**

In Rutherford's experiment, alpha particles were fired at a fine gold leaf. It was found that most of them passed through with little or no deflection. It can be deduced that:

A   Alpha particles have a positive charge.
B   Gold atoms are nearly all empty space.
C   Alpha particles have good penetrating power.
D   The gold atoms have disintegrated.
E   Atoms contain electrons.

**5**

Electrons move in a circular path of radius $R$ under the influence of a magnetic field of uniform flux density. They then enter a different region where this field still acts, but in addition there is a force of constant magnitude acting in the opposite direction to their instantaneous velocity. The result of this is that the electrons start to move in a:

A   Straight line.
B   Parabolic path.
C   Circular path of radius smaller than $R$.
D   Circular path of radius larger than $R$.
E   Path of continually decreasing radius.

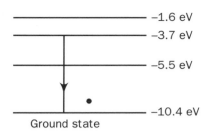

———————— −1.6 eV

———————— −3.7 eV

———————— −5.5 eV

———————— −10.4 eV

Ground state

Take

$1 \text{ eV} = 1.6 \times 10^{-19} \text{ J}$

$h = 6.6 \times 10^{-34} \text{ J s}$

$c = 3.0 \times 10^{8} \text{ m s}^{-1}$

The diagram shows the energy levels of mercury. When an electron falls from −3.7 eV to −10.4 eV the wavelength (in m) emitted will be:

A  $6.7 \times 10^{-7}$
B  $6.0 \times 10^{-26}$
C  $3.0 \times 10^{-26}$
D  $1.8 \times 10^{-7}$
E  $0.9 \times 10^{-7}$

**7**

In a demonstration of the photoelectric effect, blue light falls on a metal plate and electrons are just emitted. If the blue light is replaced by yellow light then this will:

A  Have no effect.
B  Stop the electrons being emitted.
C  Increase the rate at which electrons are emitted.
D  Decrease the rate at which electrons are emitted.
E  Increase the energy of the emitted electrons.

**8**

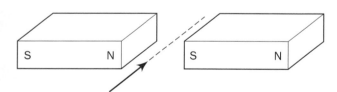

A stream of electrons follows the path shown above. The effect on the electrons is:

A  Electrons are deflected downwards.
B  Electrons are deflected upwards.
C  Electrons continue in the same direction.
D  Electrons move towards the N pole.
E  Electrons move towards the S pole.

**QUESTION**

**9**

A beam of monochromatic radiation falls on a piece of metal in a vacuum. Photoelectrons are emitted. If the intensity of the radiation is halved, the:

A    Number of emitted electrons will be doubled.

B    Number of emitted electrons will be halved.

C    Mean kinetic energy of each electron will be halved.

D    Mean velocity of each electron will be halved.

E    Maximum velocity of emitted electrons will be halved.

....................................................

**10**

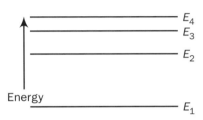

The diagram shows some energy levels in a particular atom. If an electron jump from $E_3 \rightarrow E_2$ results in emission of blue light, which jump is most likely to result in the emission of red light?

A    $E_4 \rightarrow E_3$

B    $E_4 \rightarrow E_2$

C    $E_2 \rightarrow E_1$

D    $E_3 \rightarrow E_1$

E    $E_4 \rightarrow E_1$

....................................................

# Test 17
## Units and graphs

**Time allowed:** *1 hour 20 minutes*

## Section 1: Short Questions

QUESTION 1

**(a)** Write a word equation to define electrical potential difference. Hence, or otherwise, derive an expression for the volt in terms of base units.

**(b)** Explain what is meant by homogeneity in a physical equation. Show that the equation below is homogeneous:

$$P = V^2/R$$

where $P$ is the power dissipated in a circuit element of resistance $R$ and $V$ is the potential difference across the circuit element.

2

Write down a word equation to define power. Hence express the unit of power in terms of base units. Is power a vector or a scalar quantity? Give a reason for your answer.

3

Coulomb's Law of force between electric charges may be stated in the form

$$F = Q_1Q_2/4\pi\varepsilon_0 r^2$$

Use this law to find a unit for the permittivity of free space, $\varepsilon_0$, in terms of the coulomb and base units.

A possible unit for the permeability of free space, $\mu_0$, is kg m $C^{-2}$. Show that the equation

$$c^2 = 1/\varepsilon_0\mu_0$$

where $c$ is the speed of light, is homogeneous with respect to units.

Explain why:
**(a)** An equation which is not homogeneous with respect to units must be wrong.
**(b)** An equation which is homogeneous with respect to units may nonetheless be wrong.

4

What is the difference between a vector and a scalar quantity?
Name three vector quantities and three scalar quantities.
A car travels around part of a circular path at a constant speed. Explain why the kinetic energy is conserved but the linear momentum is not.

Which of the following equations is/are homogeneous?

(a) $T = 2\pi\sqrt{r^2/g}$    (b) $gr^2 = Gm$    (c) $g = 4\pi\rho Gr^2/3$

$g$ is acceleration due to gravity;
$G$ is universal gravitational constant;
$r$ is distance;
$T$ is time period;
$m$ is mass;
$\rho$ is density.

**6**

The following equations relate to radioactive decay (with the symbols having their usual meanings).

$$dN/dt = -\lambda N \quad \text{and} \quad N = N_0 e^{-\lambda t}$$

Sketch graphs of:
(a) $dN/dt$ against $N$;
(b) $N$ against $t$;
(c) $\ln N$ against $t$.

Explain how the decay constant $\lambda$ could be obtained from two of the graphs.

**7**

A black metal sphere at temperature $T_1$ is radiating heat to its surroundings at temperature $T_2$. This situation can be described by the formula:

$$W = \sigma A\, (T_1{}^4 - T_2{}^4)$$

where $W$ is net energy per second radiated by the sphere;
$\quad A$ is surface area of the sphere;
$\quad T_1$ and $T_2$ are both temperatures;
$\quad \sigma$ is a constant.

What are the units of:
(a) $A$
(b) $T_1{}^4$
(c) $\sigma$?

Sketch a graph of $W$ against $T_1{}^4$ if all other quantities are constant.
How could you use this graph to find $\sigma$?

# Test 17

## Section 2: Multiple Choice

*Select one answer only for each question.*

**QUESTION**

**1** The units of specific heat capacity in terms of kg, m, s and K are:

- A $m^2\ s^{-2}\ K^{-1}$
- B $m^2\ s^{-2}\ K$
- C $kg\ m^2\ s\ K^{-1}$
- D $kg^2\ m\ s^2\ K^{-1}$
- E $m^2\ s^2\ K^{-1}$

**2** Which of the following is not a base unit?

- A Metre.
- B Second.
- C Mole.
- D Ampère.
- E Volt.

**3** The unit of Planck's constant is J s. This can also be written as:

- A $kg\ m^3\ s^{-2}$
- B $kg\ m^2\ s^{-2}$
- C $kg\ m\ s^{-1}$
- D $kg\ s^{-2}$
- E $kg\ m^2\ s^{-1}$

**4** Which of the following units must $X$ have for this equation to be correct?

$$Density\ =\ \frac{X}{force}$$

- A $kg\ m^{-2}\ s^{-1}$
- B $kg\ m^4\ s^{-1}$
- C $kg^2\ m^{-2}\ s^{-1}$
- D $kg\ m^3\ s^{-2}$
- E $kg^2\ m^{-2}\ s^{-2}$

**5** These are five energy formulae. In which one are base units only used?

- A Strain energy $\qquad\qquad\qquad \frac{1}{2}\ mgx$
- B Kinetic energy $\qquad\qquad \frac{1}{2}\ m\ (\Delta s/\Delta t)^2$
- C Gravitational potential energy $\quad mgh$
- D Electrical energy $\qquad\qquad\quad ItV$
- E Thermal energy $\qquad\qquad\quad mc\Delta\theta$

**6**

The relationship between two quantities $x$ and $y$ is given by $x = k/y^2$ where $k$ is a constant.

Which of the following statements obeys this relationship?

A   Magnetic flux density ($x$) at a distance ($y$) from a long straight current-carrying wire.

B   Electric field strength ($x$) at a distance ($y$) from a point charge.

C   Electric field strength ($x$) between two plates set at a distance ($y$) apart when a potential difference is applied across the plates.

D   Magnetic flux density ($x$) inside a long coil carrying a current ($y$).

E   Load ($x$) on a copper wire causing extension ($y$).

**7**

The SI unit of potential difference is equivalent to:

A   One coulomb per second.

B   One joule per coulomb.

C   One coulomb per joule.

D   One ampère per second.

E   One joule per second.

**8**

The e.m.f. ($E$) of a thermocouple is represented by:

$$E = a\theta + b\theta^2$$

where $\theta$ is temperature difference across its junctions and $a$ and $b$ are constants.
A graph of $E/\theta$ ($y$ axis) is plotted against $\theta$ ($x$ axis).
A straight line graph is obtained and its slope is:

A   $a/b$

B   $2b/a$

C   $+b$

D   $-2b$

E   $+2b$

**9**

If $p$ is the energy of a photon and $q$ is the wavelength of the corresponding radiation, which of the following is true?

A   $p = q$

B   $p = kq$ ($k$ is not $= 1$)

C   $p = k/q$

D   $p = k/q^2$

E   $p = kq^2$

**QUESTION 10**

Which of the following pairs of quantities contains one vector and one scalar?

| | | |
|---|---|---|
| A | Temperature | Speed |
| B | Force | Velocity |
| C | Work | Acceleration |
| D | Energy | Distance |
| E | Momentum | Velocity |

..........................................

**Time allowed:** *1 hour 20 minutes*

## Section 1: Short Questions

**QUESTION**

**1**

A steel ball falls vertically into a flask filled with thick oil. The ball hits the oil surface at speed and slows down almost to a halt after falling 10 cm within the oil. Show on a free-body diagram the three principal forces that act on the steel ball when it is about 5 cm below the oil surface. Explain the origin of each of these forces.

**2**

A 12 V, 24 W lamp and a resistor of fixed value are connected in some way inside a box with two external terminals. In order to discover the circuit arrangement inside the box, a student connects a variable d.c. power source and an ammeter in series with the box and obtains the following results:

| | | |
|---|---|---|
| Applied potential difference | 1.0 V | 12 V |
| Current | 1.17 A | 4.00 A |

**(a)** Draw a circuit diagram of the most likely arrangement inside the box, giving your reason.
**(b)** Use the 12 V, 4.00 A reading to deduce the value of the fixed resistor.
**(c)** What is the percentage increase in the resistance of the lamp as the applied potential difference changes from 1.0 V to 12 V?
**(d)** When the applied potential difference is increased to 24 V the current is again found to be 4.00 A. Explain this observation.

(You may neglect the internal resistance of the power supply and the resistance of the ammeter in all your calculations.)

**3**

In an alpha particle scattering experiment, an alpha particle and a gold nucleus (in a piece of gold foil) collide head-on and the alpha particle rebounds.

**(a)** Using the data below, write down a numerical expression for the electrostatic force of repulsion, $F$, acting on the alpha particle at the instant of collision when the distance between the alpha particle and the gold nucleus is $s$.

For the alpha particle $A = 4$, $Z = 2$; for the gold atom $A = 197$, $Z = 79$.
Electronic charge, $e = 1.6 \times 10^{-19}$ C.
Permittivity of vacuum $\varepsilon_0 = 8.85 \times 10^{-12}$ F m$^{-1}$.

(b) The electric potential energy of the alpha particle and the gold nucleus at the point of impact is $Fs$.
  (i)   If the initial kinetic energy of the alpha particle is 1.8 MeV, calculate a value for $s$. Assume that the gold nucleus has no kinetic energy initially (1 eV $= 1.6 \times 10^{-19}$ J).
  (ii)  What indication does the value of $s$ give about the sizes of the two particles involved?

QUESTION

4

Two long, parallel wires are mounted a distance $r$ apart. They carry currents $I_1$ and $I_2$ in the same direction. Explain why the wires attract one another.

How does this force of attraction lead to a definition of the ampère?

**5**

(a) State the principle of the conservation of energy.
(b) Define the unit in which energy is measured.
(c) The surface of Great Britain receives radiation from the sun at about 600 W m$^{-2}$. In order to design a power station with an electrical output of $2.00 \times 10^9$ W, a large area of solar panels is required.
If the conversion efficiency is only 20%, what area is this?

**6**

Optical fibres are used to transmit information using light. Explain:

(a) How a step index fibre is constructed.
(b) What is meant by material dispersion.

Calculate the time taken for light to travel along the axis of an optical fibre 20 m long if the refractive index of the core is 1.5 and that of the air is 1.0.

**7**

Explain, with reference to the behaviour of light photons, what you understand by the phrase wave-particle duality.

## Section 2: Multiple Choice

*Select one answer only for each question.*

**QUESTION 1**

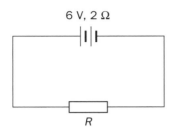

6 V, 2 Ω

R

In this circuit diagram the e.m.f. $E$ of the battery is 6 V. The internal resistance $r$ of the battery is 2 Ω.

The heat generated in the load resistor $R$ will be largest if the magnitude of $R$ is approximately:

A  ∞

B  2 Ω

C  3 Ω

D  1 Ω

E  Very, very small, i.e. zero ohms approximately.

**2–3**

A force of 10 N is applied to an object of mass 5 kg for 2 s. The object was initially at rest. The force is removed and then re-applied again as shown in the graph.

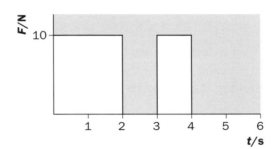

**2**

The speed of the object (in m s$^{-1}$) after 2 s is:

A  5

B  20

C  1

D  8

E  4

**3**

The speed of the object (in m s$^{-1}$) after 4 s is:

A  8

B  12

C  4

D  2

E  6

---

QUESTION
4–5

A   Newton per coulomb.
B   Newton metre.
C   Newton per kilogram.
D   Newton per square metre.
E   Newton.

Which of these could be used to measure:

4   Height of liquid × density × g.

5   Gravitational field strength.

6   On braking, 500 kJ of heat were produced when a car of total mass 1500 kg was brought to rest on a level road. The speed of the car (in $m\,s^{-1}$) just before the brakes were applied was:

A   667
B   0.667
C   25.8
D   2.58
E   6.67

7   Arranged in terms of penetrating power, starting with the most penetrating, the radiations should be listed:

A   $\alpha$   $\beta$   $\gamma$
B   $\gamma$   $\alpha$   $\beta$
C   $\gamma$   $\beta$   $\alpha$
D   $\alpha$   $\gamma$   $\beta$
E   $\beta$   $\gamma$   $\alpha$

8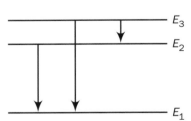

The diagram shows three energy levels for a particular atom.
In the transition $E_3 \rightarrow E_2$ radiation of wavelength $2.4 \times 10^{-7}$ m is emitted.
In the transition $E_2 \rightarrow E_1$ radiation of wavelength $10.0 \times 10^{-8}$ m is emitted.

In the transition $E_3 \rightarrow E_1$ which of the following wavelengths (in m) will be emitted?

A   $7.0 \times 10^{-8}$
B   $7.0 \times 10^{-7}$
C   $3.4 \times 10^{-7}$
D   $12.4 \times 10^{-7}$
E   $12.4 \times 10^{-8}$

**QUESTION 9**

Thermal processes and electrical processes have some common links. They are said to be analogous. Which of the following quantities are analogous?

| | | | |
|---|---|---|---|
| A | Rate of flow of energy | and | Rate of flow of charge. |
| B | Rate of flow of energy | and | Rate of flow of current. |
| C | Energy | and | Current. |
| D | Thermal conductivity | and | Electrical resistivity. |
| E | Temperature difference | and | Potential. |

**10**

A long metal wire is suspended from a fixed point and extended by a load attached to the bottom. The elastic limit has not been reached. Which of these statements is true?

| | |
|---|---|
| A | Extension at each section is proportional to its distance from the point of suspension. |
| B | Young's modulus is equal to the ratio tensile strain/tensile stress. |
| C | Tensile stress varies along the wire. |
| D | Tensile stress depends on original length of the wire. |
| E | The yield point has been reached. |

# A-Level
# Physics

# est 1

## Mechanics

Resultant force = $(200-120)$ = 80 N to RIGHT
Force = (mass)(acceleration)
Acceleration = force/mass
= 80/40
= 2 m s$^{-2}$.
To find the distance moved use:
$u = 0$; $t = 4$ s; $a = 2$ m s$^{-2}$
$s = ut + \frac{1}{2}at^2$
$= 0 + (\frac{1}{2})(2)(4)^2$
= 16 m.

**ANSWER**
**3**

$u = 0$
$s = 3.2$ m
$t = 807 \times 10^{-3}$ s
Use $s = ut + \frac{1}{2}at^2$
$3.2 = 0 + (\frac{1}{2})(a)(807 \times 10^{-3})^2$
$a = 9.83$ m s$^{-2}$.
The uncertainty is $\pm 5$ ms
If $t_1 = (807 + 5) \times 10^{-3}$ s
$t_1 = (812) \times 10^{-3}$ s
Recalculate $a_1$ ......... $a_1 = 9.71$ m s$^{-2}$
If $t_2 = (807-5) \times 10^{-3}$ s ..... $a_2 = 9.95$ m s$^{-2}$
Percentage uncertainty
$= \dfrac{(9.95 - 9.83)}{9.83} \times 100$
= 1.2%.

**4**

Force $P$ is the gravitational pull of the earth on the sphere (weight) DOWN.

The force which pairs with $P$ will also be gravitational but on the earth (not sphere) and in the opposite direction UP.

The force $Q$ is a contact force — the push of the table on the sphere UP.

The force which pairs with $Q$ will also be a contact force but on the table (not sphere) DOWN.

$F_1$ and $F_2$ are the same type (e.g. gravitational) and equal in magnitude.
$F_1$ and $F_2$ are exactly opposite in direction and act on different bodies.

$Q$ should come from the bottom of the sphere
$P$ should come from the centre of the sphere

ANSWER

5

The graph should look like this.

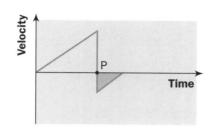

(a) The ball hits the bench at P.

(b) The force on the ball is in the same direction all the time — it is always down, due to the pull of gravity. This means that the acceleration is in the same direction as well! As the ball hits the bench (at P) the direction of its velocity changes from down to up. The graph is a velocity–time graph, so the slope of the graph is equal to the acceleration in magnitude as well as in direction. The slope of the graph is equal to $g$; it does not change direction. The magnitude of the velocity will be only half the original after the bounce because it only rebounds to half the original height.

(c) The distance the ball rises is equal to the shaded area of the graph.

6

(a) The area under a velocity–time graph is equal to the distance travelled.
Calculate the area under this graph:
$$\text{Area} = 0.5\,(10)(40) + (5)(40) + 0.5\,(5)(40)$$
$$= 500 \text{ m}.$$

(b)
$$\begin{aligned}
\text{Momentum} &= \text{mass} \times \text{velocity} \\
&= (1000)(40) \\
&= 4.0 \times 10^4 \text{ kg m s}^{-1}.
\end{aligned}$$

(c)
$$\begin{aligned}
\text{Acceleration} &= \text{change in velocity} \div \text{time} \\
&= (40 - 0) \div 10 \\
&= 4.0 \text{ m s}^{-2}.
\end{aligned}$$

(d)
$$\begin{aligned}
\text{Resultant force} &= (\text{mass})(\text{acceleration}) \\
&= (1000)(4) \\
&= 4000 \text{ N}.
\end{aligned}$$

(e) The total driving force is not the same as the resultant force. Here the resultant force causes the constant acceleration. The car is moving through air, so there is a force due to drag that increases with velocity. To keep the resultant force the same, as the drag force increases, the driving force also has to increase as shown in the diagram.

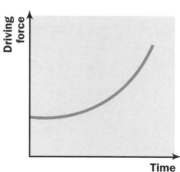

answers

Newton's Second Law of Motion states that when a resultant force is applied to a body the body will accelerate.

The acceleration will be (a) proportional to the force and (b) in the same direction as the force. The experiment must include a labelled diagram, a list of measurements, graphs plotted and conclusions drawn from the graphs.

The apparatus could be a trolley with different masses added pulled down a friction-compensated slope by different numbers of elastic cords. The acceleration could be measured with a tickertimer. Two graphs could be plotted as shown. The first graph shows acceleration ($a$) proportional to force ($F$). The second graph shows $a$ proportional to $1/m$ where $m$ is mass. So we can conclude that:

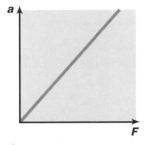
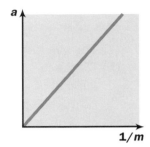

$a \propto F$

$a \propto 1/m$

$a \propto F/m$ or $F \propto ma$.

# Section 2: Multiple Choice

**A** Since the object is falling through air, there will be a viscous force (air resistance) opposing its motion. So the acceleration will not be constant. The acceleration will get smaller and smaller until the object reaches its terminal velocity, when the acceleration is equal to zero. Graph C shows velocity against time. Graph A shows acceleration against time.

**C** A car does not move forwards unless it is in contact with the road and the force must act on the car (not on the road!).

**C** Using the notation in mechanics

$$F = ma \quad \text{and} \quad v^2 = u^2 + 2as$$
$$v^2 = 2as \quad \text{since} \quad u = 0$$
$$a = v^2/2s$$
$$F = m(v^2)/2s$$

$$v^2 = \frac{2sF}{m} \quad \text{so } v \propto m^{-1/2} \text{ if } F \text{ and } s \text{ are constant.}$$

**E** Consider the UNITS of the area under the graph $m\,s^{-2} \times s \to m\,s^{-1}$. So the area must involve a velocity. Which velocity? Since we are using all the area, the answer must be E.

**5**    **A**   By Newton's Third Law, the pull on the team will be exactly equal in magnitude to the pull on the rope (but opposite in direction).

**6**    **A**   By the same reasoning as in question 5, the pull of the other team will again be 800 N.

**7**    **E**   If the lift accelerates up at 5 m s$^{-2}$ then the man will also accelerate up at 5 m s$^{-2}$. The forces on the man must produce this acceleration. The resultant force on the man must act upwards. What are the forces on the man?

$$\text{Weight } (W) = 750 \text{ N} \qquad \text{down}$$
$$\text{Contact force } (R) = \text{unknown} \qquad \text{up}$$

Since the force up is bigger than the force down

$$\text{Resultant force} = R - W \qquad \text{up}$$

By Newton's Second Law ($F = ma$)
$$R - W = ma$$
$$R - 750 = ma$$
$$R - 750 = (75)(5)$$
$$R = 1125 \text{ N}.$$

**8**    **B**

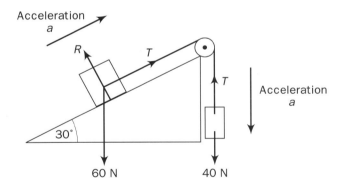

Assume a direction for the acceleration.
Both masses will have the same acceleration ($a$).

Apply Newton's Second Law ($F = ma$) to a 4 kg block
$$40 - T = 4a \qquad (1)$$
Apply the same law to a 6 kg block parallel to the plane
$$T - 60 \sin 30 = 6a \qquad (2)$$
Add (1) and (2)
$$40 - 60 \sin 30 = 10a$$
$$10 = 10a$$
$$1 = a.$$
Acceleration is 1 m s$^{-2}$ in the direction shown in the diagram.

**9**

**A** The force $F$ has to be just large enough to balance the load if there is to be no acceleration.

$$\text{The load} = 1000 \text{ N}$$
$$F = 1000 \text{ N}.$$

**10**

**D** The object has a starting velocity of $10 \text{ m s}^{-1}$. Using the usual notation:

$$u = 10 \text{ m s}^{-1}$$
$$a = 1.6 \text{ m s}^{-2}$$
$$s = 100 \text{ m}$$

and

$$v^2 = u^2 + 2as$$
$$v^2 = (10)^2 + (2)(1.6)(100)$$
$$v = 20.5 \text{ m s}^{-1}.$$

# Test 2

## Momentum and energy

## Section 1: Short Questions

**ANSWER 1**

Elastic collision
     – kinetic energy is conserved;
     – momentum is conserved.

Inelastic collision
     – kinetic energy is not conserved;
     – some kinetic energy is changed to other forms.

NB Total energy is conserved in all collisions (from the classical point of view).

**(a)** Bullet embedded in target:
    1  Inelastic;
    2  Kinetic energy → sound of bullet;
                            → heat;
                            → energy used to deform target material.

**(b)** Gas molecules colliding:
    1  Elastic;
    2  All energy stays as kinetic although it may be redistributed amongst the particles.

**(c)** Ionising collision:
    1  Inelastic;
    2  Kinetic energy of particle
                       → electrostatic potential energy to electron and positive ion;
                       → kinetic energy to electron;
                       → kinetic energy to positive ion;
                       → some kinetic energy left with beta particle.

  In this collision the air molecule is split into an electron and a positive ion.

  Some energy is used to carry out this process (called ionisation).

**2**

As the particle approaches it has a large velocity ($v$). The gold nucleus exerts a repulsive force so the particle will slow down (velocity decreases). When the two particles are close together the force will be very large and $v$ zero. The particle will rebound and its velocity will increase again but in the opposite direction.

The slope of this graph ($\Delta v/\Delta t$) = acceleration.
The force on the particle is in the same direction all the time.
The acceleration is in the same direction all the time.

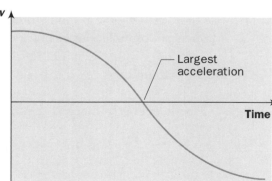

If the ball is originally moving to the right
Momentum = (mass)(velocity)
= (0.16)(35)
= 5.6 kg m s$^{-1}$ to the right.

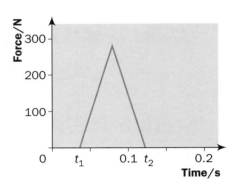

You can see the force is changing from zero at $t_1$ to 280 N at 0.08 s and back to zero at $t_2$:

(a) Average force = (0 + 280)/2
= 140 N.
(b) Impulse = average force × time
= (140)(0.12 – 0.04)
= 11.2 N s.
(c) Impulse = change in momentum
$Ft = mv - mu$ (but watch the signs!)
Take movement to right as positive.
The force is to the left
(−140)(0.08) = (0.16)$v$ − (0.16)(+35)
TO LEFT         TO RIGHT
−11.2 + 5.6 = 0.16$v$
−35 m s$^{-1}$ = $v$     i.e. ball moves to left
Speed of ball finally is 35 m s$^{-1}$.

(a) Inelastic – all the kinetic energy of the bullet is NOT changed into gravitational potential energy.
(b) Yes – momentum is always conserved. What are the necessary conditions?
(c) No – see above.
(d) Kinetic energy = 0.5 (mass)(velocity)$^2$
= 0.5 (0.05)(88)$^2$
= 194 J.
(e) Momentum = (mass)(velocity)
= (0.05)(88)
= 4.4 kg m s$^{-1}$.
(f) Use the conservation of momentum.
Momentum of bullet before collision = momentum of block AND bullet after collision
(0.05)(88) = (0.05 + 1.50)$v$
We want to find $v$:     $v$ = (0.05)(88)/(0.05 + 1.50)
= 2.8 m s$^{-1}$.
(g) Kinetic energy of block and bullet = gravitational potential energy of block and bullet
(0.5)(1.55)(2.8)$^2$ = (1.55)(9.8)($h$)
$h$ = (0.5)(1.55)(2.8)$^2$/(1.55)(9.8)
= 0.40 m.

**ANSWER**

**5**

It is foolish not to wear a seat belt. Why?

Newton's First Law states:

A body (in this case the child) will continue in a straight line unless a force acts to stop it. If there is no force exerted by the seat belt then the child will go straight on until it hits something like the windscreen. The driver, however, will be held back by the seat belt and stop with the car. In other words the child is injured but the driver is not.

The car has a given amount of momentum that has to be reduced to zero.

Newton's Second Law states:

Force $\times$ time $=$ change in momentum

If the change in momentum is fixed then the longer the time the smaller the force will be. Cars are designed to increase the time of the collision, e.g. crumple zones, rubber bumpers, air bags.

**6**

Kinetic energy $= (0.5)(9.0 \times 10^{-31})(10^6)^2 = 4.5 \times 10^{-19}$ J.

Momentum $= (9.0 \times 10^{-31})(10^6) = 9.0 \times 10^{-25}$ kg m s$^{-1}$.

Kinetic energy is scalar (no direction).

Momentum is vector (this has direction).

Scalar quantities – speed, temperature, power.

Vector quantities – velocity, acceleration, force.

**7**

**(a)** Momentum is conserved in all collisions and explosions provided that:

(i) A specific direction is considered.

(ii) No other forces act in that direction except those involved in the collision itself.

**(b)** Momentum of A before collision $= (1.6)(0.6) = 0.96$ kg m s$^{-1}$

Momentum of B before collision $= (0.8)(0.10) = 0.08$ kg m s$^{-1}$

Total momentum of A and B $= 0.96 + 0.08 = 1.04$ kg m s$^{-1}$

Momentum of A after collision $= (1.6)(0.37) = 0.59$ kg m s$^{-1}$

Momentum of B after collision $= (0.8)(0.57) = 0.46$ kg m s$^{-1}$

Total momentum of A and B $= 0.59 + 0.46 = 1.05$ kg m s$^{-1}$

These two answers are close enough to say momentum is conserved. To identify the type of collision we must calculate the total kinetic energy before and after the collision. If kinetic energy is the same in both cases then the collision is elastic, but if it is not the same the collision is inelastic. Make these calculations to find out which type of collision occurred.

## Section 2: Multiple Choice

**1**

**C** Elastic collision is a special type of collision in which the total kinetic energy of all particles involved is not changed to other forms of energy; the total momentum stays the same and so does the total energy.

**ANSWER**

**2**

**B** If the ball rebounds to exactly the same height, then just after it leaves the metal plate it has exactly the same kinetic energy as it had before the collision. Kinetic energy is conserved – elastic collision.

**3**

**A** If $m$ is the mass and $v$ the velocity

$$\begin{aligned}\text{Kinetic energy} &= \tfrac{1}{2}\,mv^2 \\ &= (\tfrac{1}{2})(100 \times 10^{-3})(6)^2 \\ &= 1.8 \text{ J.}\end{aligned}$$

**4**

**B** Energy is measured in joules or newton metres

A  gives $(N\,m\,s^{-1})$

B  gives $(N\,m^{-2})(m^3) = N\,m$

C  gives $(N)(m\,s^{-2})$

D  gives $(kg)(m\,s^{-2})$

E  gives $(kg)(m\,s^{-1})$.

**5**

**C** If $m$ is mass and $v$ is velocity

$$\begin{aligned}\text{Kinetic energy} &= (\tfrac{1}{2})\,mv^2 \\ &= (\tfrac{1}{2})(1000)(10^2) \\ &= 5 \times 10^4 \text{ J}\end{aligned}$$

$$\begin{aligned}\text{Momentum} &= mv \\ &= (1000)(10) \\ &= 1 \times 10^4 \text{ kg}\,m\,s^{-1}.\end{aligned}$$

**6**

**D** Using the usual notation

$$\text{Average force on balls} = \frac{mv - mu}{t} \text{ from Newton's Second Law}$$

$$= \frac{m}{t}(v - u) \text{ where } \frac{m}{t} \text{ is mass per second}$$

$$\text{Mass per second} = (0.4)(600)/10 = 24 \text{ kg}\,s^{-1}$$

Since velocity is a vector, if $u = +15 \text{ m}\,s^{-1}$

$$v = -15 \text{ m}\,s^{-1}$$

Average force on balls = $24(-15 - 15) = -720$ N (i.e. in same direction as $v$)

Average force on walls $\quad = +720$ N (in same direction as $u$).

**7**

**B** Apply the conservation of momentum to the disintegration.

Before disintegration total momentum = 0

After disintegration total momentum = 0

Momentum of $\alpha$ particle in one direction = momentum of thorium nucleus in opposite direction, i.e.

(mass of $\alpha$)(speed of $\alpha$) = (mass of thorium)(speed of thorium)

$$\frac{\text{speed of }\alpha}{\text{speed of thorium}} = \frac{234}{4}$$

**8**

**E** Momentum $p = mv$

$$p^2 = m^2v^2$$

$$\frac{p^2}{m} = \frac{m^2v^2}{m}$$

$$= mv^2$$

$$= \text{kg } (\text{m s}^{-1})^2$$

$$= \text{kg m}^2 \text{ s}^{-2}.$$

Which answer matches this?

Try E $\quad$ J $= \text{N m}$

$$= (\text{kg m s}^{-2})(\text{m})$$

$$= \text{kg m}^2\text{s}^{-2}.$$

**9**

**B** Apply conservation of momentum.

Momentum before $= (4m)(0) + (2m)(5)$

Momentum after $= (6m)(v)$

$$6mv = 10m$$

$$v = 10/6 = 5/3.$$

**10**

**C** Percentage efficiency $=$ (useful power/power put in ) $\times 100$

Useful power $=$ (force $\times$ distance)/time

$$= (200 \times 16)/4$$

$$= 800 \text{ W}$$

Power put in $= 1000 \text{ W}$

Percentage efficiency $= (800/1000) \times 100 = 80\%.$

**est 3**
# Circular motion, rotation and gravitation

## Section 1: Short Questions

**ANSWER**

**1**

**(a)** These are the only forces acting on the skater.

$W$ – pull of earth on skater (weight)
$R$ – push of ice on skater (contact force)
$F$ – frictional force on skater by ice (friction)

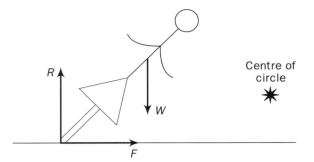

**(b)** Centripetal force is the essential force for circular motion (towards centre). Here it is produced by $F$, the frictional force.

$$F = \frac{mv^2}{r}$$

$$= \frac{(70)(7.0)^2}{10}$$

$$= 343 \text{ N.}$$

**2**

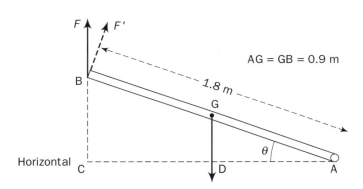

**(a)** The bonnet rotates about A because A is the fulcrum.
Take moments about A.

If the bonnet is in equilibrium:
Moment clockwise due to $F$ = moment anticlockwise due to weight

$$F \times \text{length AC} = mg \times \text{length AD}$$
$$F \times (1.8 \cos \theta) = (12)(9.8) \times 0.9 \cos \theta$$
$$F = 59 \text{ N.}$$

NB When taking moments always use the perpendicular distance from the fulcrum.

(b) (i) Take moments about A again.

Moment clockwise due to $F'$ = moment anticlockwise due to weight

$$F' \times \text{length AB} = mg \times \text{length AD}$$
$$F' \times (1.8) = (12)(9.8) \times 0.9 \cos 24$$
$$F' = 54 \text{ N.}$$

(ii) Since $F = 59$ N and $F' = 54$ N

$$F > F'$$

It must be easier to apply force in direction of $F$.

**ANSWER**

**3**

(a) Gravitational force ($F$) acting on an astronaut mass $m$ pulls him towards the centre of the earth (mass $M$).
By the universal law of gravitation,
$F = G\,m\,M/d^2$ where $d = R + h$
$F = G\,m\,M/(R + h)^2$
In low orbit $h << R$ so force $F$ is not affected very much by $h$. So in low earth orbit, force will only be slightly less than if the astronaut was standing on earth.

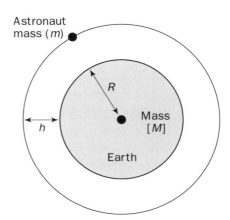

(b) Weightlessness occurs because the weight of the astronaut is just sufficient to provide the centripetal force and maintain the orbit. The reaction on the astronaut is zero.

NB There is still a resultant force acting on the astronaut – his weight. Weightlessness does not mean 'no weight'!

**4**

(a) The centripetal force $mv^2/r$ is produced by the pull of the earth on the spacecraft. The earth's pull is the weight $mg'$.

$$mg' = mv^2/r$$
$$g' = v^2/r$$
$$9.4 = v^2/(6560 \times 10^3)$$
$$v = \sqrt{(9.4 \times 6560 \times 10^3)} = 7850 \text{ m s}^{-1}.$$

(b) The time period $T$ can be found from the total distance travelled divided by the velocity.
$T = 2\pi(6560 \times 10^3)/7850 = 5250$ s.
Notice the units here! Since $g$ is in m s$^{-2}$ all distances must be in metres also.

**5**

Robert's weight is balanced by the tension in the rope.
Tension $= mg = 20 \times 9.8 = 196$ N.

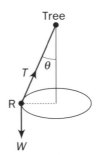

When he swings in a circular path the vertical component of the tension balances the weight. This is shown in the above diagram.

If $T$ is the new tension, then $T \cos \theta = mg$

$$T = mg / \cos \theta$$
$$T = (20 \times 9.8)/(0.66) = 296 \text{ N}.$$

**ANSWER**

**6**

(a) The four forces are:
1  Weight – pull of earth on aeroplane
2  Lift – force up due to motion of aeroplane through the air
3  Thrust – pull forward by the engines
4  Drag – friction between aeroplane and the air.

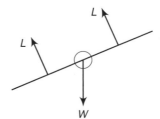

(b) When the aeroplane turns, the wings are tilted at an angle to the horizontal. The component of the lift provides the force towards the centre.

**7**

When the mass is at the bottom of the circle, the tension acts in the opposite direction to the weight. We need a resultant force towards the centre of the circle so the tension must be bigger than the weight.

$$T_1 - mg = mv^2/r$$

Hence $T_1 = (mv^2/r) + mg$

When the mass is at the top of the circle, the tension acts in the same direction as the weight. We still need the same centripetal force so the two forces together must now produce $mv^2/r$.

$$T_2 + mg = mv^2/r$$

Hence $T_2 = (mv^2/r) - mg$

You can see that $T_1$ is bigger than $T_2$.

Maximum tension occurs at the bottom of the circle.

Minimum tension occurs at the top of the circle.

## Section 2: Multiple Choice

**ANSWER**

**1**

**B** Don't be misled! Be sure of your facts! The satellite does not have constant velocity. The satellite has an acceleration towards the centre of $v^2/d$ where $v$ is velocity, $d$ is the radius. The satellite has a centripetal force of $mv^2/d$. The time period is $2\pi d/v$. Its velocity does not double if radius doubles. If $M_E$ is the mass of the earth:

Since $\dfrac{mv^2}{d} = \dfrac{GmM_E}{d^2}$      so      $v^2 = \dfrac{GM_E}{d}$

So    $v^2 \propto \dfrac{1}{d}$          or as radius increases velocity gets smaller.

**2**

**D** If $v$ is velocity, $r$ radius and $T$ is time for one rotation:

Circular orbit      $v = \dfrac{2\pi r}{T}$

$$v = \frac{2\pi(1.5 \times 10^{11})}{365 \times 24 \times 3600}$$

$$v = 3.0 \times 10^4 \text{ m s}^{-1}.$$

**3**

**D** Circular orbit.

Acceleration   $= \dfrac{v^2}{r}$

$$= \frac{(3.0 \times 10^4)^2}{1.5 \times 10^{11}}$$

$$= 6.0 \times 10^{-3} \text{ m s}^{-2}.$$

**4**

**B** Circular motion always involves changing velocity (but the speed – a scalar quantity – can remain constant). If the velocity is changing there must be an acceleration and of course if there is an acceleration then there must be a force!

**5**

**E** The two forces form a couple and the torque of the couple $= Fd$.

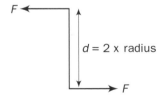

So the torque on the cylinder $= (0.2)(40 \times 10^{-2})$
$$= 0.08 \text{ N m}.$$

---

**6**    **E**    The work done by a force is calculated using (force × distance).
The work done by a couple is calculated using (torque × angle).
For one rotation the angle is $2\pi$ radians.
Work done = $(0.08)(2\pi)$
          = 0.50 J.

**7**    **E**    The conker is pulled in by the string. The string is pulled in by the girl's hand but the girl's hand is pulled out by the string. The speed of the conker does not change (scalar) but velocity of the conker is changing (vector). When the string is cut the force producing the circular motion will cease to exist. The conker will carry on in its original path – along the tangent. Its velocity does not change – it stays the same!
Incorrect statement?

**8**    **B**    For circular motion

$$\text{Acceleration} = \frac{v^2}{r} \qquad \text{where } v \text{ is velocity}$$
$$r \text{ is radius}$$

$$\text{Time period } T = \frac{2\pi r}{v}$$

$$v = \frac{2\pi r}{T}$$

$$\text{Acceleration} = \left(\frac{2\pi r}{T}\right)^2 \div r$$

$$= \frac{4\pi^2(10)^2}{25} \div 10$$

$$= 1.6\pi^2.$$

**9**    **A**    For circular motion

$$F = \frac{mv^2}{r} \quad \text{and} \quad v = \frac{2\pi r}{T} \qquad \text{where } r = \text{radius}$$
$$m = \text{mass}$$
$$v = \text{velocity}$$
$$T = \text{time period}$$

$$F = \frac{m}{r} \frac{4\pi^2 r^2}{T^2}$$

$$F = \frac{m\,4\pi^2 r}{T^2}$$

$$= \frac{(2)(4)(\pi^2)(5)}{4^2}$$

$$= (5/2)\,\pi^2\,\text{N}.$$

**10**    **C**    For circular motion, acceleration towards the centre (radial acceleration)
is usually written as $r\omega^2$, where $\omega = $ angular velocity.
If $v$ is the linear velocity, $\omega = v/r$
$r = v/\omega = 3.0/0.6 = 5$ m
So the radial acceleration $= r\omega^2 = (5)(0.6)^2$
$= 1.8$ m s$^{-2}$.

## Test 4
# Simple harmonic motion

## Section 1: Short Questions

**ANSWER**
**1**

**(a)** Simple harmonic motion is a periodic motion in which the acceleration is:
  – towards the centre of the motion;
  – proportional to the displacement from the centre.
Notice that the definition must be in terms of acceleration. Nothing else will do!

**(b)** Examples of simple harmonic motion could be:
  1  pendulum oscillating
  2  spring oscillating
  3  tuning fork oscillating
  4  guitar string oscillating

NB  Windscreen wipers or any types of circular motion would not be acceptable examples.

**(c)**

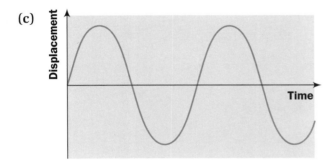

**2**

Acceleration $\propto -x$ (from the definition)
If velocity is denoted by $v$ then     $v^2 = \omega^2(x_0^2 - x^2)$
Kinetic energy is $K$ then       $K = \frac{1}{2}mv^2$
where $\omega = 2\pi/T$,
  $T$ is time period
  $m$ is mass
  $x$ is displacement
  $x_0$ is the amplitude
The graphs will look like this.

**(a)**

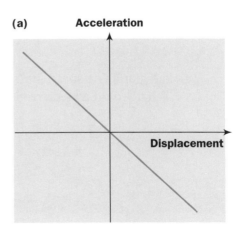

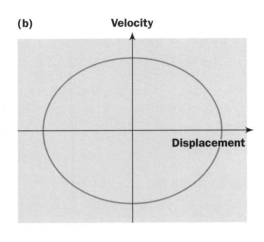

**(b)** Velocity / Displacement

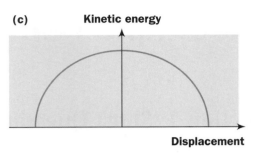

**(c)** Kinetic energy / Displacement

**ANSWER**

**3**

This is simple harmonic motion applied to a spring.

Static extension (with load) = 0.31 m = $e$

Amplitude = 0.06 m = $a$

For an oscillating spring,

$$\text{Time period } (T) = 2\pi\sqrt{(e/g)}$$
$$= 2\pi\sqrt{(0.31)/(9.81)}$$
$$= 1.12 \text{ s.}$$

$$\text{Frequency } (f) = 1/T$$
$$f = 1/1.12$$
$$= 0.89 \text{ Hz.}$$

**(a)** Amplitude (maximum displacement) = 0.06 m (given)

**(b)** Hence displacement per scale division = 0.06/3
$$= 0.02 \text{ m}$$

**(c)** OA represents half of one time period

From above $T = 1.12$ s

$$T/2 = 0.56 \text{ s}$$

OA represents 0.56 s.

**4**

**(a)** The graph is a speed–time graph. Since speed is a scalar there are no negative values. (What would a velocity–time graph look like?)

For simple harmonic motion.

$v_{max} = \omega x_0$ where $\omega = 2\pi/$time period $(T)$ and $x_0$ = amplitude

From the graph

$v_{max} = 0.25 \text{ m s}^{-1}$ and $T = 4.0$ seconds

$x_0 = v_{max}/\omega$

$$= 0.25/\frac{2\pi}{4.0}$$

$$= 0.16 \text{ m.}$$

**(b)** Average speed $= \dfrac{\text{total distance travelled}}{\text{time taken}}$

$= \dfrac{\text{area under speed–time graph}}{\text{time taken}}$

One way to find the area is to count the squares.
Approximate number of squares (1 cm × 1 cm) = 24
From the scale, 1 square $= (0.05 \text{ m s}^{-1})(0.5 \text{ s})$

$= 0.025 \text{ m}$

Hence, average speed $= \dfrac{(24)(0.025)}{4.0}$

$= 0.15 \text{ m s}^{-1}.$

**(c)** Average velocity is zero since average displacement is zero!
NB Velocity is a VECTOR quantity.

**ANSWER**

**5**

The largest force occurs when there is the largest acceleration.
Use $F = ma$, so $0.064 = (0.100)(a_{max})$

$a_{max} = 0.64 \text{ m s}^{-2}$
$0.64 = \omega^2 x_0$
$= \omega^2 (20 \times 10^{-3})$
$\omega^2 = 32$ so $\omega = 5.7$

**(a)** $v_{max} = \omega x_0 = (5.7)(20 \times 10^{-3}) = 0.11 \text{ m s}^{-1}.$
**(b)** $T = 2\pi/\omega = 2\pi/5.7 = 1.1 \text{ s}.$

**6**

A simple pendulum is one which is assumed to have all its mass in the bob, the string having none.
A pendulum which measures seconds will have a time period equal to 2 seconds.
Using the formula $\qquad T = 2\pi\sqrt{(l/g)}$

$2 = 2\pi\sqrt{(l/9.8)}$

$\dfrac{4 \times 9.8}{4\pi^2} = l = 0.99 \text{ m}.$

If the pendulum was taken to the moon, $T$ would increase since the magnitude of $g$ is smaller $(9.8/6) \text{ m s}^{-2}$. Make the calculation if you do not believe it!

**7**

Simple harmonic motion is defined in terms of acceleration.
Acceleration $= |\omega^2 x|$ where $\omega = 2\pi/T.$
Since $\omega$ is a constant then $T$ must also be constant.

We need an experiment to show the time period does not change.
Apparatus required would be a simple pendulum, firmly clamped so it cannot move, and a stop watch.

Set the pendulum swinging through a small angle.
Time the first 20 oscillations. Call this $T_1$.
Time the second 20 oscillations. Call this $T_2$.
Time the third 20 oscillations. Call this $T_3$.
If $T_1 = T_2 = T_3$ then the oscillation is simple harmonic motion.

## Section 2: Multiple Choice

ANSWER
1

**D**  On the earth, time period of pendulum $T$

$$T = 2\pi\sqrt{\frac{l}{g}} \qquad\qquad (1)$$

On the moon, time period of pendulum $T'$

$$T' = 2\pi\sqrt{\frac{l}{g/6}} \qquad\qquad (2)$$

Divide (2) by (1) to obtain $T'$

$$\frac{T'}{T} = 2\pi\sqrt{\frac{l}{g/6}} \bigg/ 2\pi\sqrt{\frac{l}{g}}$$

Cancel!

$$\frac{T'}{T} = \sqrt{\frac{1}{1/6}}$$

$$\frac{T'}{T} = \sqrt{6}$$

$$T' = \sqrt{6}\,T$$

2–3

For simple harmonic motion you must use specialised formulae. Learn them!

Velocity ($v$) at displacement ($x$) is given by $v^2 = w^2(x_0^2 - x^2)$
where $w = 2\pi/T$
and $x_0$ = amplitude.

2

**B**  Maximum velocity will occur at the centre ($x = 0$)

$$v_{max}^2 = w^2\,(x_0^2 - 0)$$

$$= \left(\frac{2\pi}{0.10}\right)^2 (2.0)^2$$

$$v_{max} = 126 \text{ cm s}^{-1}.$$

3

**B**  Velocity when $x = 1.0$ cm

$$v^2 = w^2(x_0^2 - x^2)$$

$$= \left(\frac{2\pi}{0.10}\right)^2 (2.0^2 - 1.0^2)$$

$$v = 109 \text{ cm s}^{-1}$$

4

**D**  There are only two forces acting on the pendulum bob. These are the tension and the weight.

**ANSWER**

**5**

**B**   For a simple pendulum

$$T = 2\pi\sqrt{\frac{l}{g}}$$

$$T^2 = \frac{4\pi^2 l}{g}$$

∴ $\quad 2\log T = \log\left(\frac{4\pi^2}{g}\right) + \log l$

∴ $\quad 2\log T - \log\left(\frac{4\pi^2}{g}\right) = \log l$

$$mx + c = y.$$

**6**

**E**   During simple harmonic motion the acceleration ($a$) and the displacement ($x$) are in antiphase.

$$\text{acceleration} = -(\text{constant}) \times (\text{displacement})$$
$$a = -k\,x$$

The phase difference is in radians.

**7**

**D**   The acceleration will be largest when the displacement is largest. Similarly both will be minimum at the same time.

**8**

**C**   Frequency $(f) = \dfrac{1}{\text{time period } (t)}$

From the graph, the time of one full oscillation $(t) = 20$ ms

$$f = \frac{1}{20 \times 10^{-3}}$$
$$= 50 \text{ Hz.}$$

**9**

**B**   Amplitude $(x_0)$ is the maximum displacement from the mean position, i.e. 4 $\mu$m.

**10**

**C**   This is simple harmonic motion with maximum velocity at the centre of the vibration.

$$\text{Maximum velocity} = (2\pi f)(x_0)$$
$$= (2 \times \pi \times 50)(4)$$
$$= 400\pi.$$

## Section 1: Short Questions

**ANSWER**

**1**

Steel has a rigid crystalline structure so a large tensile force ($F_1$) is required to extend it by a small amount. The applied force has to increase the separation of the molecules (stretch the bonds).

Rubber molecules are long and coiled so a relatively small force ($F_2$) will uncoil them, thus increasing the length of the rubber much more easily.

When the steel wire is in the form of a spring, the coiled structure is similar to that of a rubber molecule. A large amount of elastic potential energy can be stored, since the same average force as above ($F_1$) will now produce a much larger extension.

NB Elastic potential energy stored = (average force) × (extension).

**2**

(a) As $r$ decreases from $r_0$ the force becomes a repulsive force which gets larger and larger. When $r$ is small the force is very large indeed.

(b) As $r$ increases from $r_0$ the force becomes an attractive force which increases to a maximum value and then decreases. When $r$ is very large the force is still attractive but tending towards zero.

The separation value $r_0$ is when the resultant force is zero. Any attractive or repulsive forces cancel out.

**3**

(a) For steel  Young's modules(Y.M.) = stress/strain

$$2.0 \times 10^{11} = \text{stress}/0.0002$$
$$\text{stress} = 0.0004 \times 10^{11} = 4.0 \times 10^{7} \, N\,m^{-2}$$

For polythene  Y.M. = stress/strain
$$3.0 \times 10^{7} = \text{stress}/0.0002$$
$$\text{stress} = 6.0 \times 10^{3} \, N\,m^{-2}$$

(b)
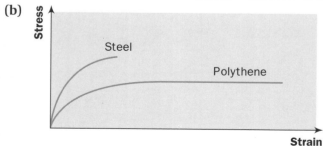

(c) Extension $= \dfrac{\text{force}}{\text{Y.M.}} \times \dfrac{\text{length}}{\text{area}}$

$$= \dfrac{(10)(2)}{(2.0 \times 10^{11})\pi(1 \times 10^{-3})^2}$$

$$= 3.2 \times 10^{-5} \text{ m}$$

(d)  Strain $=$ extension/length

$$= \text{force}/(\text{Y.M.} \times \text{area})$$

$$= 10/(3.0 \times 10^7)(0.2 \times 10^{-5})$$

$$= 0.17.$$

**ANSWER**

**4**

(a) $T = 2\pi\sqrt{(e/g)} = 2\pi\sqrt{(0.010)/(9.8)}$

$$= 0.2 \text{ s.}$$

(b) $v =$ amplitude $\times \omega$ (where $\omega = 2\pi/T = 10\pi$)

$$= (0.005)(10\pi) = 0.16 \text{ m s}^{-1}.$$

(c) Kinetic energy $= \frac{1}{2}(\text{mass})(\text{maximum velocity})^2$

$$= 0.5(0.010)(0.16)^2$$

$$= 1.3 \times 10^{-4} \text{ J.}$$

**5**

(a) It is difficult to extend a metal bar because the molecules exert a force opposing the extension. This means the molecules must be attracting one another.

(b) Similarly, it is difficult to compress a metal bar because the molecules oppose the compression by repelling one another. The conclusion is that molecules can both attract and repel one another.

**6**

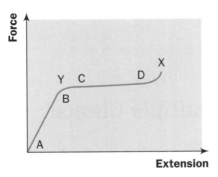

(a) Elastic region is where the wire will return to its original shape and size when the weights are removed (A–B).

(b) Plastic region occurs after the elastic region. A large extension occurs for a small increase in force (C–D).

(c) Breaking point is the point where the wire breaks! In other words enough force has been applied to pull the molecules apart (X).

(d) Yield point is the point where the plastic region starts (Y).

(e) Area under the graph represents the work done in stretching the wire or the elastic energy stored in the stretched wire.

NB For the Hooke's Law region, this is the area of a triangle.

**ANSWER**

**7**

(a) Young's modulus, $E$ = tensile stress/tensile strain.

(b)

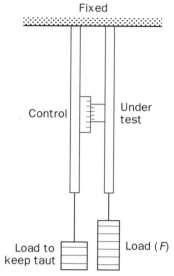

(c) Measurements to be made:

   1  Original length of the wire, $L$, using metre rule.

   2  Diameter of wire, $d$, using a micrometer.

   3  Weights added to bottom of wire, $W$.

   4  Extension of wire for each weight, $e$, using a vernier scale

(d) $E$ = tensile stress/tensile strain; so a graph of tensile stress against tensile strain will have a slope equal to $E$. For each set of results:

Calculate tensile stress = $W / \dfrac{\pi d^2}{4}$

Calculate tensile strain = $e/L$

Plot the above graph and measure its slope $E$. Units?

# Section 2: Multiple Choice

**1**

**A**  This is about Young's modulus ($E$) where: $E = \dfrac{F}{A} \div \dfrac{e}{L}$

Since $e/L$ is the strain                  strain = $F/EA$

($F$ is load, $A$ cross sectional area)         = $F/E\pi r^2$

For the first wire of radius $r$       strain 1 = $F/E\pi r^2$

For the second wire of radius $2r$    strain 2 = $F/E\pi(2r)^2$

                    Strain 2 ÷ strain 1 = $F/E\pi(2r)^2 \div F/E\pi r^2$

                               = $\frac{1}{4}$

                 so strain 2 = $\frac{1}{4} \times$ strain 1

**2**

**A**  Strain has no units.

    Strain = $\dfrac{\text{extension (m)}}{\text{original length (m)}}$

**3** **C** Young's modulus $(E)$ $= \dfrac{\text{(force)}\,\text{(length)}}{\text{(extension)}\,\text{(area)}}$

$$= \dfrac{(15)(10)}{(0.1 \times 10^{-3})(\pi)(1.6 \times 10^{-3})^2}$$

$$= 1.87 \times 10^{11}\,\text{N}\,\text{m}^{-2}.$$

**4** **C** Young's modulus $(E)$ $= \dfrac{\text{force}(F) \times \text{length}(L)}{\text{area}(A) \times \text{extension}(x)}$

extension $(x)$ $= \dfrac{FL}{AE}$

Increasing $(x)$ would require:
(i) larger load; or
(ii) longer length; or
(iii) smaller area; or
(iv) smaller Young's modulus.

**5** **A** You will notice that the graph is a 'loop' which does not join up. This means the sample does not return to its original length, nor does it break. The slope of the graph changes so Young's modulus cannot be constant, since the slope of a stress–strain graph is equal to Young's modulus. Since there is an enclosed area, some energy must be dissipated. Hence the correct answer is A.

**6** **E** The slope of a stress–strain graph is equal to Young's modulus.
Since stress = force/area and strain = extension/length, the correct graph has to be E.

**7** **B** From the definition of Young's modulus $E = FL/xA$
Look back to question 4 to see what the terms mean!
For wire A $\quad x_A = FL/EA = mgL/E\pi r^2$
For wire B $\quad x_B = mg(2L)/E\pi(2r)^2$
$x_A / x_B = mgL/E\pi r^2 \div mg(2L)/E\pi(2r)^2$
$= 1 \div 2/4 = 2.$

**8** **B** Change each quantity into base units, starting with pressure.
Pressure = force/area = $\text{kg}\,\text{m}\,\text{s}^{-2}/\text{m}^2$ = $\text{kg}\,\text{m}^{-1}\,\text{s}^{-2}$.
A Strain = extension/length so has no units.
B Energy/volume = force × distance/volume
$= \text{kg}\,\text{m}^2\,\text{s}^{-2}/\text{m}^3 = \text{kg}\,\text{m}^{-1}\,\text{s}^{-2}$.
We do not need to look any further (unless you want the practice!).

**9**

**C** We go back to question 4 again to find the equation (or use question 7).
Extension = $FL/EA$
(i) Steel wire is harder to stretch not easier – copper is more ductile.
(ii) Smaller load means smaller $F$ and less extension.
(iii) Thinner wire has smaller wire area and larger extension.
(iv) Shorter wire means smaller $L$ and less extension.
(v) Lower temperature means stretching is not so easy.

**10**

**D** Call the thin wire number 1 and the thicker wire number 2.
Since the extensions are the same we can write

$$F_1L_1/E_1\pi\frac{d^2}{4} = F_2L_2/E_2\pi\frac{(2d)^2}{4}$$

but $F_1 = F_2$ and $L_1 = L_2$.
The denominators of these equations are equal:

$$E_1\pi\frac{d^2}{4} = E_2\pi\frac{4d^2}{4}$$

$$\frac{E_1}{4} = E_2.$$

est 6

answers

# Geometric optics and progressive waves

## Section 1: Short Questions

**ANSWER**

**1**

Use a protractor and draw a good diagram to scale. Put arrows on the rays to show the direction of the light.

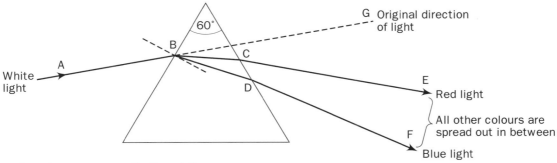

**Refraction** occurs at B, C and D.

The light rays change speed at these points (slow down at B and speed up again at C and D). The bending associated with refraction is due to this change in speed.

### Deviation

The original direction of the light (ABG) has been changed to ACE for red light and ADF for blue light. This change in direction is called the deviation.

### Dispersion

The white light has been spread out into its constituent colours because the different colours (or wavelengths) do not all travel at the same speed in glass. This spreading out is called dispersion. The blue is deviated the most.
Remember BLUE BENDS BEST (for prisms!).

**2**

A progressive wave is one in which energy travels from source to surroundings.
The wave travels slower in the shallow water. The critical angle will occur in the shallow water where the speed is slower. (Compare with light — critical angle occurs in denser medium where speed is slower.)

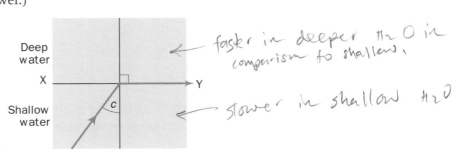

fasker in deeper H₂O in comparism to shallans.

slower in shallow H₂O

$$\frac{\sin c}{\sin 90} = \frac{\text{speed in shallow water}}{\text{speed in deep water}}$$

$$\sin c = \frac{0.20}{0.26} = 0.77$$

$$c = 50.3°.$$

Refraction can be demonstrated with water waves in a ripple tank. A piece of glass is inserted in part of the bottom of the tank thus making the water shallower. A long ruler dips regularly into the water at X.

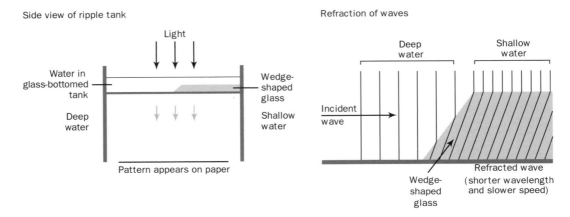

ANSWER

3

(a) Multimode optical fibre: This is a very pure glass fibre which transmits light signals by total internal reflection. The light can take many different paths. This is what multimode means – many ways.

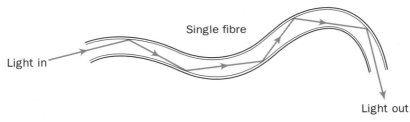

(b) Step index optical fibre: The fibre has two parts, the core and the cladding. In this fibre there is a sudden change between the refractive index of these two parts.

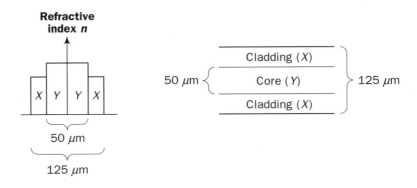

(c) Attenuation of the signal: The intensity of the signal will be reduced due to several factors, e.g. absorption of energy by the medium. This is what attenuation means.

**ANSWER**

**4**

The equation to use is $n_1 \sin \theta_1 = n_2 \sin \theta_2$
where $n_1 = 1.00$ and $n_2 = 1.5$
$\theta_1$ is the angle of incidence in air and $\theta_2$ is angle of refraction in glass.

Calculate $\sin \theta_2$ from $(\frac{1.00}{1.50} \times \sin \theta_1)$

| $\theta_1/°$ | $\sin \theta_1$ | $\sin \theta_2$ | $\theta_2/°$ |
|---|---|---|---|
| 0 | 0 | 0 | 0 |
| 20 | 0.34 | 0.23 | 13 |
| 40 | 0.64 | 0.43 | 25 |
| 60 | 0.87 | 0.58 | 35 |
| 90 | 1.00 | 0.67 | 42 |

With this information the required graphs can be plotted.

**5**

(a) A wave is the movement of energy from source to surroundings. In a longitudinal wave the oscillations are along the direction of the energy. In a transverse wave the oscillations are at 90° to the direction of energy. You could draw two diagrams here.

(b) Longitudinal waves: sound, compression waves in a rod, ultrasound.
Transverse waves: water waves, light, radio.
You could quote a slinky spring for either of these.

(c) This is an example of the inverse square law. If the distance is doubled the intensity falls by $1/(2d)^2$; that is, by one quarter.

**6**

(a) Electromagnetic spectrum.

(b) Light has the shorter wavelength.

(c) Both waves can be reflected (bounced off things). Both waves can be refracted (change speed in media of different density).

(d) Apparatus required is shown in the diagram below.

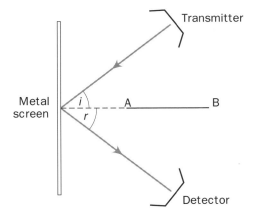

The source is a microwave oscillator. The detector picks up the waves.
The path of the waves is not distinct since they spread out — they are detected over a large angle. The maximum signal is noted. The barrier AB is placed to prevent the waves taking a short cut across from source to detector. The law of reflection can be proved by measuring the angles using a protractor.

ANSWER

7

A mechanical wave uses the oscillations of the material itself to transfer energy. An electromagnetic wave does not use the medium at all. The energy is transferred by means of oscillating electric and magnetic fields. Water waves and sound waves are examples of mechanical waves. Water waves can be demonstrated using a ripple tank. Sound waves can be shown using a loudspeaker.

## Section 2: Multiple Choice

**1**

**C** You must learn these because this should be an easy question.
The whole sequence starting with smallest wavelength (largest frequency) is:
$\gamma$ – X – ultraviolet – blue light – red light – infra-red – microwaves – radio waves.

**2**

**E** This is about a progressive wave. One wavelength is the shortest distance apart of two points in phase, but within one wavelength the two points with zero displacement will be only half a wavelength apart. This is shown on the displacement–time graph below.

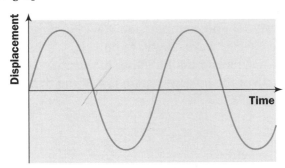

To calculate wavelength use $v = f\lambda$.
$$\lambda = v/f = 5/10 = 0.5 \text{ m.}$$

Therefore the shortest distance between two points with zero displacement is 0.25 m.

**3**

**B** For any wave
Speed $(v)$ = frequency × wavelength
$$320 = 200 \times \lambda$$
$$1.6 \text{ m} = \lambda$$
Two points 0.4 m apart are $\lambda/4$ apart.

Path difference $\lambda \rightarrow$ phase difference $2\pi$
Path difference $\lambda/4 \rightarrow$ phase difference $\pi/2$.

**4**

**D** Sound waves CANNOT be polarised.
Sound waves CAN interfere destructively.
Longitudinal waves CAN be diffracted.
Electromagnetic waves CAN be diffracted.
Stationary waves ARE NOT always transverse.

The true statement is D.

**ANSWER**

**5**  C  The wave travels slower in the shallow water so the wave bends towards the normal as it leaves the boundary. Angle $\theta_2$ will be smaller than angle $\theta_1$. (If total internal reflection occurred it would be in the shallow water.)

**6**  B  X-rays have a short wavelength and high frequency. Infra-red rays have a longer wavelength and lower frequency. Both travel at the same speed in a vacuum.

**7**  C  Polarisation is the property which distinguishes transverse waves from longitudinal waves. Longitudinal waves cannot be polarised. Transverse waves can be polarised.

**8**  D  Refraction occurs as the light travels from air to perspex. This means a change in speed occurs along with a change in wavelength. The frequency does not change.

**9**  A  If $\alpha$ is bigger than $c$ then total internal reflection will occur. No light will be transmitted.

**10**  A  The air is less dense than the glass. The air has a smaller refractive index. The light will be bent away from the normal since it travels faster in air.

# Test 7

## Wave properties

# Section 1: Short Questions

**ANSWER 1**

The diagram must be labelled.

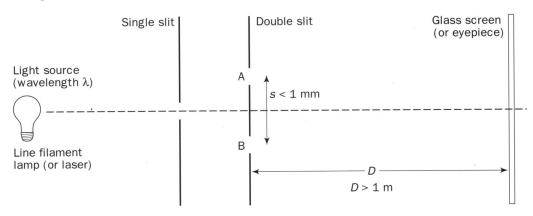

**(a)** Diffraction occurs at each slit.

Waves from slit A and slit B overlap.

An interference pattern occurs in the region of overlap.

If more diffraction occurs the pattern will be wider since the region of overlap is wider.

More diffraction occurs if $(\lambda / s)$ is large.

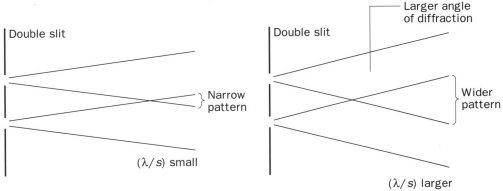

**(b)** The principle of superposition states that the resultant displacement due to the waves from slits A and B depends on the sum of the individual displacements. If the two waves meet in phase (in step) bright light will be seen since the displacements add up.

This occurs if the path difference $= n\lambda$ where $(n = 0, 1, 2...)$.

If the two waves meet completely out of step (antiphase) then no light will be seen since the displacements cancel out. This occurs if the path difference $= (n + {}^{1}/_{2})\lambda$.

Summary: Diffraction affects the width of the pattern. Superposition affects the appearance of the pattern.

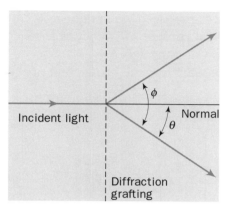

Incident light | Normal

$\phi$

$\theta$

Diffraction grafting

(a) For a diffraction grating
$$d \sin \theta = n\lambda$$
First order spectrum if $n = 1$
$$d \sin \theta = \lambda$$
Number of lines/metre on grating is $N$ where $N = 1/d$
$$1/d = N = \sin \theta / \lambda$$
But $\theta = 46°43'/2$
$$N = \frac{\sin (46°43'/2)}{644 \times 10^{-9}}$$
$$= 615\,700 \text{ lines/metre.}$$

(b) For second order spectrum
$$n = 2$$
$$d \sin \theta = 2\lambda$$
$$\frac{1}{615\,700} \sin \theta = 2(644 \times 10^{-9})$$
$$\sin \theta = 0.8.$$
Since $\sin \theta < 1$ the second order is visible.

Simple harmonic motion is a periodic motion in which:
(i) acceleration is proportional to the displacement from the mean position;
(ii) acceleration is always towards the mean position.

Use
$$f = \frac{1}{2l} \sqrt{\frac{T}{\mu}}$$
$$= \frac{1}{2 \times 30 \times 10^{-2}} \sqrt{\frac{70}{5 \times 10^{-3}}}$$
$$= 197 \text{ Hz}$$
where $f$ is frequency;
$l$ is length of string;
$T$ is tension of string;
$\mu$ is mass/unit length for the string.

'Damped' means the oscillating string is losing energy, mainly due to air resistance.
The kinetic energy and stored potential energy in the string are dissipated as sound. The amplitude of the motion decreases with time.

**(a)** Plane polarised light is produced when ordinary light passes through a piece of polaroid. Ordinary light consists of vibrations at random in all planes perpendicular to the direction of travel of the light.

In polarised light the vibrations are confined to one plane.

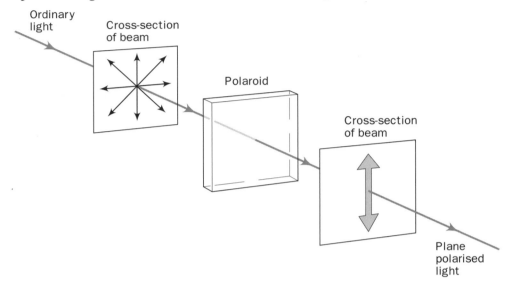

**(b)** Brewster's Law states that reflected light can be completely plane polarised if the angle of incidence is a very specific magnitude, i.e. when $\tan \theta_p = n$.

We need to measure $\theta_p$ and $n$

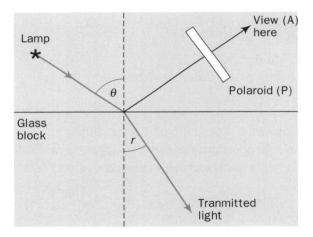

The reflected light is viewed at (A) through (P). Watch the intensity of the light as (P) is rotated. For one angle of incidence ($\theta_p$) the intensity will fall to zero as (P) is rotated. When this occurs the reflected beam is plane polarised.

Record $\theta_p$ and $r$ using a protractor.

Calculate $n = \sin \theta_p / \sin r$.

Calculate $\tan \theta_p$.

If $\tan \theta_p = n$ then Brewster's Law is true.

(a) For water waves, use the ripple tank shown below. Young's two slit experiment demonstrates interference. Here the two slits are made using pieces of metal.

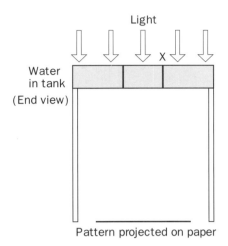

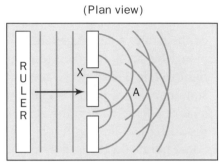

(Plan view)

A is the area where interference occurs

Pattern projected on paper

The sizes of the slits are about the same size as the wavelength of the wave. The waves interfere where they meet. If two crests meet – constructive interference. If a crest and a trough meet – destructive interference.

(b) For microwaves, use apparatus based on the same idea of two slits. Here the slits are one or two centimetres apart. The aerial will pick up places with high intensity signals (constructive interference) and some with low intensity signals (destructive interference).

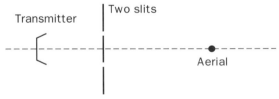

**6**

(a) Velocity of a wave is the speed at which the energy travels through the medium.
(b) Wavelength of a wave is the shortest distance between two points which are in phase.
(c) Look at the diagram below. At the centre of XY the sound will be maximum. As M moves along XY it will pass through alternate maxima and minima (loud/soft).

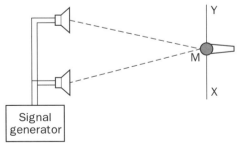

Principle of superposition states that when two or more waves travel through the same medium at the same time then they will superimpose such that the resultant is the algebraic sum of the two displacements.
The effect with the two loudspeakers depends on the magnitude of the path difference.

If $x = 0, \lambda, 2\lambda$, etc. — maximum,
If $x = \lambda/2, 3\lambda/2, 5\lambda/2$, etc. — minimum,
For maximum $x = n\lambda$; for minimum $x = (n + \frac{1}{2})\lambda$.

**ANSWER**

**7**

A stationary wave on a stretched string could be set up as shown below. An oscillator is connected to a signal generator. This arrangement allows a progressive wave to travel along the string from left to right. An exactly similar wave will be reflected back from right to left. These two waves interfere and for certain frequencies will produce a stationary wave pattern. The signal generator allows the frequency of the oscillation to be changed. The load on the end of the string can also be varied. For certain arrangements the string will look as if it is not moving. The wave profile is stationary.
Some points on the string do not move at all. These points are called nodes. The nodes are half a wavelength apart.

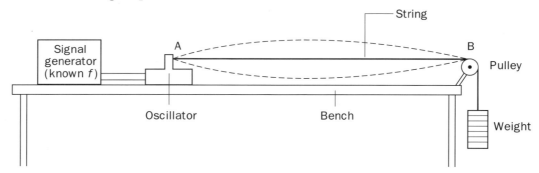

# Section 2: Multiple Choice

**1**

**B** For a stretched string oscillating at its fundamental frequency

$$f = \frac{1}{2l} \sqrt{\frac{T}{\mu}} \qquad (1)$$

If $T$ and $l$ are both halved (keeping $\mu$ constant) the new frequency

$$f' = \frac{1}{2(l/2)} \sqrt{\frac{T/2}{\mu}} \qquad (2)$$

Divide (2) by (1)

$$\frac{f'}{f} = \frac{1}{2(l/2)} \sqrt{\frac{T/2}{\mu}} \div \frac{1}{2l} \sqrt{\frac{T}{\mu}}$$

$$= \frac{2}{2l} \sqrt{\frac{T/2}{\mu}} \times \frac{2l}{1} \sqrt{\frac{\mu}{T}}$$

$$= 2\sqrt{\frac{1}{2}}$$

$$= \sqrt{2}.$$

**ANSWER**

**2**

**A** You know the formula

$$x = \frac{D\lambda}{s}$$

where $x$ is the fringe separation;
$D$ is the distance from double slits to screen;
$\lambda$ is the wavelength of the light;
$s$ is the separation of the double slits.
Check all the answers to see what happens to the magnitude of $x$.

**3**

**A** Remember both progressive and stationary waves can be transverse or longitudinal. Answer A is not true since the displacement of particles in a transverse progressive wave would be perpendicular to the direction of energy travel. In a longitudinal stationary wave the displacement would be parallel to the direction of energy travel. Answers B – E correctly state the situation.

**4**

**E** Longitudinal waves cannot be plane polarised. All waves can be reflected.

**5**

**A** $d \sin \theta = n\lambda$ where $d$ is the grating spacing;
$n$ is order of spectrum;
$\lambda$ is wavelength of light.

Number of lines $\text{mm}^{-1} = 600$
Number of lines $\text{m}^{-1} = 600 \times 10^3$

$$d = \frac{1}{600 \times 10^3} \text{ m}$$

$$= 1.67 \times 10^{-6} \text{ m}.$$

Since $n = 2$ $\quad \sin \theta = \dfrac{2\lambda}{d}$

$$= \frac{(2)(6.0 \times 10^{-7})}{1.67 \times 10^{-6}}$$

$$= 0.718$$

$$\theta = 46°.$$

**6**

**D** Frequency $(f) = 300$ Hz
Velocity $(v) = 6000 \text{ m s}^{-1}$

$$\text{Wavelength } (\lambda) = \frac{v}{f} = \frac{6000}{300} = 20 \text{ m}$$

If the wavelength of this travelling wave is 20 m then 2.5 m represents $\lambda/8$.

A phase change of $2\pi$ is equivalent to $\lambda$

$$2\pi/8 \text{ is equivalent to } \frac{\lambda}{8}.$$

**ANSWER**

**7**

**D** A phase difference of $\pi/2$ radians is equivalent to $\lambda/4$.
(NB $2\pi$ radians $\cong \lambda$)

**8**

**E** For a wire vibrating with fundamental frequency ($f$) $f = \dfrac{1}{2l}\sqrt{\dfrac{T}{\mu}}$
where $l$ = length;
$T$ = tension.

$$\mu = \frac{\text{mass}}{\text{length}}$$

$$= \frac{\text{density} \times \text{volume}}{\text{length}}$$

$$= \frac{\text{density} \times (\text{area} \times \text{length})}{\text{length}}$$

$$= \text{density} \times \text{area}$$

$$= \rho \times A$$

$$f = \frac{1}{2l}\sqrt{\frac{T}{\rho A}}.$$

But $A = \pi r^2$ where $r$ = radius

$$f = \frac{1}{2l}\sqrt{\frac{T}{\rho \pi r^2}}.$$

Since $l$, $T$, $\rho$, $\pi$ are all constants, by rearranging we get

$$f = \frac{1}{2l}\sqrt{\frac{T}{\rho \pi}} \times \sqrt{\frac{1}{r^2}}$$

or $f = k(^1/r)$

For wire (1)   $f_1 = k(^1/2)$ i.e. $2f_1 = k$
For wire (2)   $f_2 = k(^1/1)$ i.e. $f_2 = k$
i.e.       $2f_1 = f_2$.

**9**

**B** This is a displacement–time graph.
The speed is equal to the slope of this graph.
The speed will be zero where the slope is zero i.e. at $t$ = 0, 4, 8 seconds.

**10**

**B** When $t$ = 2 seconds the displacement is zero.
The graph represents simple harmonic motion.
The acceleration is zero when the displacement is zero.

# Test 8

## Temperature and internal energy

### Section 1: Short Questions

**ANSWER**

**1**

A length of 20.0 cm is equivalent to 100°C.
A length of 0.2 cm is equivalent to 1.0°C.
A length of $(0.2 \times 16)$ cm is equivalent to 16°C.
A length of $(0.2 \times 5.0)$ cm is equivalent to 5°C.

(a) The mark will be 3.2 cm above the 0°C mark.
(b) The mark will be 1.0 cm below the 0°C mark.

**2**

(a) Conservation of energy.
(b) $\Delta U$ is the change in internal energy.
$\Delta Q$ is the extra thermal energy added to or removed from the system.
$\Delta W$ is the work done by or on the system.
(c) There is no change in internal energy $\therefore \Delta U = 0$.

**3**

(a) Mercury-in-glass thermometer uses linear expansion.
(b) Platinum resistance thermometer uses change in electrical resistance.
(c) Constant-volume air thermometer uses change in pressure.

**4**

(a) Thermal equilibrium means an object is losing heat to its surroundings and gaining heat from its surroundings at the same rate.
(b) The junction maintains a constant temperature.
(c) A thermocouple is used to measure temperature in a nuclear reactor.
(d) The thermocouple has a small heat capacity so it reacts quickly. It also measures temperature at a point and can be read remotely.

**5**

Refer back to question 2 where the meaning of the terms is given.
$\Delta U$ is zero since the bulb is at a constant temperature.
$\Delta Q$ is heat being given out from the bulb.
$\Delta W$ is the work being done on the bulb, i.e. the electrical input.
So here $\Delta Q = -\Delta W$.

**ANSWER**

**6**

Here 100°C is equivalent to $(3.780 - 3.500)\,\Omega$, i.e. $0.280\,\Omega$,
so $1.0°C$ is equivalent to $0.280/100$, i.e. $2.8 \times 10^{-3}\,\Omega$,
or $1.0\,\Omega$ is equivalent to $100/0.280\,\Omega$, i.e. $357°C$.
Hence $(3.620\,\Omega - 3.500\,\Omega)$ or $0.120\,\Omega$ is equivalent to $(357 \times 0.12)°C$
Answer then is $43°C$.
Perhaps you prefer to use the formula

$$\frac{t}{100} = \frac{X_t - X_0}{X_{100} - X_0}$$

Advantages would be accuracy and a remote control facility.

**7**

First the thermocouple has to be calibrated, using the apparatus below.

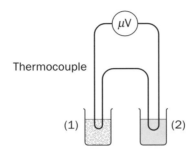

With both junctions in ice the microvoltmeter reads zero. With junction (1) in ice and junction (2) in steam, meter reads $X_{100}$. The thermocouple is now calibrated, meaning we know what the readings mean! Now proceed to find the temperature of the oil. With junction (1) in ice and junction (2) in oil, meter reads $X_t$. To calculate the temperature $t$ record $X_{100}$, $X_t$ and substitute in

$$\frac{t}{100} = \frac{X_t - X_0}{X_{100} - X_0} \qquad \text{where } X_0 \text{ is zero.}$$

# Section 2: Multiple Choice

**1**

**D** $\qquad \dfrac{t}{100} = \dfrac{l_t - l_0}{l_{100} - l_0} \qquad$ where $l_{100} = 200$ mm and $l_t = 48$ mm.

If $t = 20°C$

$$\frac{20}{100} = \frac{48 - l_0}{200 - l_0}$$

Rearrange to find $l_0$

$$20(200 - l_0) = 100(48 - l_0)$$
$$4000 - 20l_0 = 4800 - 100l_0$$
$$l_0 = 10 \text{ mm.}$$

**2**

**C** For an ideal gas the internal energy $(U)$ is the total kinetic energy of all the molecules

$$PV = nRT = \tfrac{1}{3} Nmc^2$$

$$3nRT = Nmc^2.$$

Divide both sides by 2

$$\tfrac{3}{2}nRT = N(\tfrac{1}{2}mc^2)$$

$$\tfrac{3}{2}nRT = U$$

$$\therefore \quad U \propto T.$$

So a graph of $U$ against $T$ is a straight line through the origin.

**ANSWER**

**3**

**B** Average energy $= 3kT$
$$= 3(1.38 \times 10^{-23})300$$
$$= 1.24 \times 10^{-20} \text{ J}.$$

**4**

**C** The First Law of Thermodynamics is another way of stating the conservation of energy.
$$\Delta U = \Delta Q + \Delta W$$
where $\quad \Delta U =$ change in internal energy;
$\quad \Delta Q =$ thermal energy added or removed;
$\quad \Delta W =$ work done by or on the system.
Do not be misled by the other answers. For example, temperature may remain constant and this law can be used to explain what happens – but the law itself simply tells you that ENERGY IS CONSERVED.

**5**

**D** For an isothermal expansion there is no change in temperature and hence no change in the internal energy ($U$)
$$\Delta U = 0.$$

**6**

**C** A change in internal energy is always associated with a change in temperature. In situation C the temperature remains the same. There will be no net change in the internal energy. In all the other given situations the temperature will change.
In A the gas does work – it will cool.
In B the gas is heated – temperature rises.
In D the pressure is constant – not the temperature.
In E the gas is cooled.

**7**

**D** Try the thermopile!
(Do you know how it works?)

**8**

**D** You could not use a mercury-in-glass thermometer if the pond is deep!

**9**

**C** Use the formula $\dfrac{t}{100} = \dfrac{X_t - X_0}{X_{100} - X_0}$  where $X_0 = 0$

$$X_{100} = 5.00\,\text{mV}$$
$$X_t = ?$$
$$t = 60°\text{C}$$

Substitute  $\dfrac{60}{100} = \dfrac{X_t}{5.00}$  Watch the units.

**10**

**D** To measure any temperature all of these are important except D. A high thermal capacity would mean the thermometer would take a lot of heat from the system and in so doing reduce the temperature you are trying to measure!

# Test 9
## Using thermal energy

## Section 1: Short Questions

**ANSWER 1**

Thermal energy will flow from the transistor to the surroundings by three methods.

1   Conduction – thermal energy is passed along the material, transmitted by the vibrations of the molecules.
2   Convection – thermal energy is transferred in fluids; as the fluid becomes hot it becomes less dense and therefore rises. Colder, more dense, fluid sinks down to take its place and the process is repeated.
3   Radiation – energy travels as electromagnetic waves (infra-red), not using the medium at all.

Make sure that you link these to the design features!

1   The transistor is attached to metal. Since metal is a good conductor the thermal energy will be conducted away.
2   The metal has a large surface area (fins) so a lot of air is heated and convection will occur.
3   The dull black metal is a good radiator of heat – and the large area will increase the rate of heat flow.

**2**

Read accurately from the graph and redraw it very carefully.

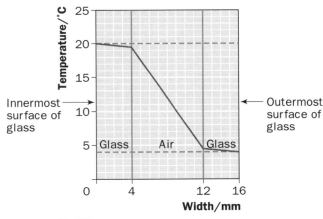

The air is a poorer conductor than the glass so the temperature drop/mm is more across the air (the line is steeper). Since both pieces of glass are the same thickness, the temperature drop across both is the same (0.5°C).

To find the average temperature gradient use a straight line graph.

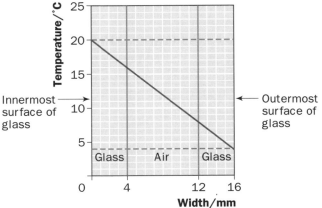

Use $\Delta Q/\Delta t = (k)(A)(\Delta\theta/\Delta x)$

$120 = (k)(1)(20 - 4)/(16 \times 10^{-3})$

$k = 0.12 \text{ W m}^{-1}\text{ K}^{-1}$.

**ANSWER**

**3**

This is about thermal conductivity.

$$\frac{\Delta Q}{\Delta t} = kA\frac{\Delta\theta}{\Delta x} \quad \text{where } \frac{\Delta Q}{\Delta t} \text{ is the power loss}$$

$$= \frac{(0.04)(40)(18 - 6)}{100 \times 10^3} = 192 \text{ W}.$$

If the thickness of the fibreglass is doubled, the power loss will be halved to 96 W. In a hot summer the temperature outside is higher than the temperature inside, so heat tends to flow into the house. The fibreglass will reduce this heat flow and the house will stay cooler.

**4**

Not as complicated as it looks!

Heat transfer through a bar – thermal conductivity.

$$\frac{\Delta Q}{\Delta t} = kA\frac{\Delta\theta}{\Delta x}$$

$$= \frac{(385)(1.50 \times 10^{-4})(100)}{12.0 \times 10^{-2}} = 48 \text{ W}.$$

Now $\Delta Q = (L)(m)$, so in 15 seconds

$(48)(15) = (3.34 \times 10^5)(m)$

$m = 2.15 \times 10^{-3} \text{ kg}$.

Assume all the heat transferred through the bar is used to melt the ice (none is lost through the sides). Calculated amount might be:

**(a)** Higher than amount melted in practice due to heat gained from the outside (which is at higher temperature).

**(b)** Lower than amount melted in practice due to heat lost through the sides of the bar (lagging will not be perfect).

**5**

**(a)** Heat capacity = mass × specific heat capacity, so for four discs:

Heat capacity = $4 \times 3.0 \times 500 = 6000 \text{ J K}^{-1}$.

**(b)** Kinetic energy of the car is converted into heat energy in the brakes.

Kinetic energy of car = $\frac{1}{2}Mv^2 = \frac{1}{2}(1000)(40^2) = 8.0 \times 10^5 \text{ J}$

This energy is shared between the four brakes.

One brake receives one quarter of this energy, i.e. $2.0 \times 10^5 \text{ J}$

For one brake: $2.0 \times 10^5 \text{ J} = mc\,\Delta\theta$

$$\Delta\theta = 2.0 \times 10^5 \text{ J}/(3.0)(500) = 133°C.$$

**ANSWER**

**6**

(a) Look carefully at the graph.

From A to B the solid is being heated. All the energy is being used to increase the oscillations of the molecules, i.e. to increase their kinetic energy.

At B the solid starts to change into a liquid. The energy is used to rearrange the molecules, increasing their potential energy.

At C all the solid has changed into a liquid. From C to D the liquid is being heated and the molecules receive kinetic energy again.

(b) The temperature is constant because all the energy is being used to change the state of the material. This energy is called latent heat (hidden heat).

(c) From A to B temperature rises by 40°C in 4 minutes and there is 1 kg of material. The rate of heating is 2000 J every minute, so in 4 minutes total energy received is 8000 J.

$$\Delta Q = mc\Delta\theta$$
$$8000 = (1)(c)(40) \qquad c = 200 \text{ J kg}^{-1}\text{K}^{-1}.$$

(d) From B to C there is no rise in temperature, but in 3 minutes the energy received is still 6000 J. What is it used for? It provides the latent heat.

$$\Delta Q = m L$$
$$6000 = (1)(L) \qquad L = 6000 \text{ J kg}^{-1}.$$

**7**

Devise any experiment which will find the heat capacity of a calorimeter. Do you know what heat capacity is? The following experiment would do! Use the method of mixtures, i.e. heat a block of copper in a beaker of boiling water. Quickly transfer it into the calorimeter which contains some cold water.

Record the following measurements.

1  Mass of copper $m$;
2  Mass of cold water $M$;
3  Temperature of boiling water $\theta_B$;
4  Temperature of cold water $\theta_C$;
5  Temperature of mixture $\theta_M$.

You will also need to know specific heat capacity of copper $c$ and of water $c_W$.

If the heat lost by the copper = heat gained by water and calorimeter

$$mc(\theta_B - \theta_M) = Mc_W(\theta_M - \theta_C) + H(\theta_M - \theta_C)$$

Hence calculate $H$, the heat capacity of the calorimeter.

Did you know $H$ = mass of calorimeter × specific heat capacity of material of which it is made?

# Test 9

## Section 2: Multiple Choice

**ANSWER**

**1**    **B**   This is about thermal conductivity. We shall call the unknown temperature at the interface $\theta/^\circ C$.

For conduction of heat

$$\frac{\Delta Q}{\Delta t} = kA\frac{\Delta\theta}{\Delta x} \qquad \text{where } \frac{\Delta Q}{\Delta t} \text{ is the rate of heat flow in J s}^{-1}.$$

$$\frac{\Delta Q}{\Delta t} \text{ for bar } P = \frac{\Delta Q}{\Delta t} \text{ for bar } Q$$

$$kA\frac{\Delta\theta}{\Delta x} \text{ for } P = kA\frac{\Delta\theta}{\Delta x} \text{ for } Q$$

$$kA\frac{(100 - \theta)}{2 \times 10^{-3}} = 40\,kA\frac{(\theta - 0)}{20 \times 10^{-3}}$$

Calculate out to find $2000 = 100\theta$.

**2**    **E**   If $m$ is the mass of the water, $c$ its specific heat capacity and $\Delta\theta$ its change in temperature, then heat required

$$\begin{aligned} &= mc\,\Delta\theta \\ &= (\text{volume})(\text{density})(c)(\Delta\theta) \\ &= (0.15)(1000)(4200)(40) \\ &= 2.52 \times 10^7 \text{ J}. \end{aligned}$$

**3**    **E**   If $Q$ is heat produced, $m$ is mass of the water, $c$ its specific heat capacity and $\Delta\theta$ is the rise in temperature, then $Q = mc\,\Delta\theta$.

For the first mass of water, heat produced in 2 minutes

$$Q = (0.10)(c)(10)$$

Heat produced per second

$$\begin{aligned} &= \frac{(0.10)(c)(10)}{2 \times 60} \\ &= (8.33 \times 10^{-3})(c) \text{ J}. \end{aligned}$$

For the second mass of water, the heat required

$$\begin{aligned} Q' &= (0.05)(c)(15) \\ &= (0.75)(c) \text{ J}. \end{aligned}$$

So time required in the second instance

$$\begin{aligned} \frac{Q'}{Q} &= \frac{0.75c}{(8.33 \times 10^{-3})(c)} \\ &= 90 \text{ s}. \end{aligned}$$

**ANSWER**

**4**

**C** Reducing fuel bills means reducing the rate of flow of heat $\frac{\Delta Q}{\Delta t}$ from the house. The rate of heat flow through the glass and through the layer of still air will be the same once the steady state has been reached.

$$\frac{\Delta Q}{\Delta t} = kA\frac{\Delta \theta}{\Delta x} \text{ for glass is same as } \frac{\Delta Q}{\Delta t} = kA\frac{\Delta \theta}{\Delta x} \text{ for air}$$

where $k$ = thermal conductivity;
$\quad\quad A$ = area;
$\quad\quad \Delta \theta$ = temperature difference;
$\quad\quad x$ = thickness.

Since the thermal conductivity ($k$) of air is about 1/40 that of glass, then increasing the thickness of the air will have the largest effect.

**5**

**D** There are three stages of heating here. Each stage has to be calculated independently.

1. Changing the ice into water
   Heat required = (mass)(latent heat of fusion)
   $$Q_1 = (0.050)(3.2 \times 10^5)$$
   $$= 1.60 \times 10^4 \text{ J.}$$

2. Heating the water from 0°C to 100°C
   Heat required = mass × specific heat capacity × change in temperature
   $$Q_2 = (0.050)(4200)(100)$$
   $$= 2.1 \times 10^4 \text{ J.}$$

3. Changing the water into steam
   Heat required = (mass)(latent heat of vaporisation)
   $$Q_3 = (0.050)(2.3 \times 10^6)$$
   $$= 11.50 \times 10^4 \text{ J.}$$

Total heat required
$$= Q_1 + Q_2 + Q_3$$
$$= 15.2 \times 10^4$$
$$= 1.52 \times 10^5 \text{ J.}$$

**6**

**B** For thermal conduction

$$\frac{\Delta Q}{\Delta t} = kA\frac{\Delta \theta}{\Delta x} \text{ where } \frac{\Delta Q}{\Delta t} = \text{rate of heat flow per second}$$

where $k$ = thermal conductivity;
$\quad\quad A$ = area of cross section;
$\quad\quad \Delta \theta$ = temperature difference;
$\quad\quad \Delta x$ = length.

For bar A $\quad \frac{\Delta Q}{\Delta t} = (25)(1.0 \times 10^{-4})\left(\frac{60-40}{40 \times 10^{-2}}\right)$

$$= 12.5 \times 10^{-2} \text{ W.}$$

For bar B $\dfrac{\Delta Q}{\Delta t} = (25)(4.0 \times 10^{-4})\left(\dfrac{60 - 40}{40 \times 10^{-2}}\right)$

$= 50.0 \times 10^{-2}$ W.

Total rate of heat flow $= 0.125 + 0.50$

$= 0.625$ W.

**ANSWER**

**7**    **A**   The kinetic energy of the bullet $(\frac{1}{2}mv^2)$ is transferred into heat $(mc\,\Delta\theta)$

$\frac{1}{2}mv^2 = mc\,\Delta\theta$

$\dfrac{v^2}{2c} = \Delta\theta$

$\dfrac{(250)^2}{2(130)} = \Delta\theta$

$240 = \Delta\theta.$

Maximum temperature $= 240 + 300$

$= 540$ K.

**8**    **D**   This uses the same formula as question 6 above.
The symbols have the same meanings.

$$\dfrac{\Delta Q}{\Delta t} = kA\dfrac{\Delta\theta}{\Delta x}$$

$$\dfrac{\Delta Q}{\Delta t}\Big/A = k\dfrac{\Delta\theta}{\Delta x}$$

$$\dfrac{\Delta Q}{\Delta t}\Big/A \text{ for brick} = p \times \dfrac{\Delta Q}{\Delta t}\Big/A \text{ for glass}$$

so $\quad k\dfrac{\Delta\theta}{\Delta x}$ for brick $= p \times k\dfrac{\Delta\theta}{\Delta x}$ for glass.       (1)

But $\Delta\theta$ is the same for both and $\dfrac{k}{\Delta x}$ is the same for both as well!

Also $k$ for brick is $\frac{1}{6}k$ for glass $\therefore\ k_B = \frac{1}{6}k_G$
and $\Delta x$ for brick is $50 \times \Delta x$ for glass, $\therefore\ \Delta x_B = 50\Delta x_G$.

Substitute these values in equation (1)

Use $\dfrac{k}{\Delta x}$ for brick $= p\dfrac{k}{\Delta x}$ for glass

$$\left(\frac{1}{6}k_G\frac{1}{50\Delta x_G}\right) = p\left(k_G\frac{1}{\Delta x_G}\right)$$

$$1/300 = p.$$

**9**    **A**   This question is about thermal conductivity $(k)$. In a cavity wall the still air is an excellent insulator. The temperature drop across the air will be large.
The brick is a much better conductor. The temperature drop across the brick will be smaller.

**10**    **D**   Since steady state has been reached the rate of heat flow is the same all through the wall.

# Test 10
## Gases

## Section 1: Short Questions

**ANSWER 1**

This experiment appears in many textbooks.

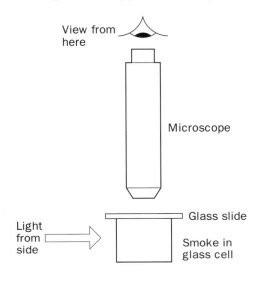

View from here

Microscope

Light from side

Glass slide

Smoke in glass cell

Smoke is introduced into the glass cell using a burning straw and the apparatus set up as shown.

Bright specks of light are seen moving erratically – these are smoke particles being bombarded unevenly on all sides by (invisible) air molecules. Since the particles are very light, the bombarding air molecules transfer energy to them and they move around. The motion of the smoke particles is observed through the microscope and explained by considering air as made up of many particles in constant, random motion.

**2**

$$PV = nRT$$

where $n$ is the number of moles;
        $R$ is molar gas constant.

'Estimate' means a sensible guess. Assume volume of 100 W light bulb is 150 cm³.

**(a)** $P$ = $1.0 \times 10^5$ Pa;
  $T$ = $(17 + 273)$ K;
  $R$ = $8.3$ J mol⁻¹K⁻¹;
  $\mu$ = $(40 \times 10^{-3})$ kg;
  $PV = nRT$;

  $PV = \dfrac{m}{\mu}RT$ where $m$ is mass of gas;
              $\mu$ is molar mass (mass of one mole).

$$(1.0 \times 10^5)(150 \times 10^{-6}) = \frac{(m)}{(40 \times 10^{-3})}(8.3)(17 + 273)$$

$$m = 2.5 \times 10^{-4} \text{ kg.}$$

# Test 10

**(b)** When the lamp has been switched on for some time the temperature of the gas is 57°C.

For constant volume
$P_1/T_1 = P_2/T_2$

$$P_2 = P_1 T_2/T_1$$
$$= (1.0 \times 10^5)(273 + 57)/(273 + 17)$$
$$= 1.14 \times 10^5 \text{ Pa}.$$

ANSWER

**3**

**(a)** Velocity is a vector quantity and can vary in
1  magnitude;
2  direction.

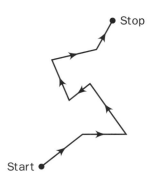

This diagram shows six collisions.
The motion of the molecule is random in direction, its speed varies at random and so does the distance apart of the molecules.

**(b)** Work done = pressure × (change in volume)          (1)
A gas is more compressible than a liquid; therefore a small change in pressure will produce a much larger change in volume in a gas than in a liquid.
Referring to equation (1) above:
For same change in pressure
$(V)_{\text{gas}} > (V)_{\text{liquid}}$
$P(V)_{\text{gas}} > P(V)_{\text{liquid}}$          ($P$ constant)
Work done on gas > work done on liquid.

**4**

**(a)** Kinetic theory assumptions could be:
1  There are no forces between molecules except when they collide.
2  All collisions are elastic.
3  The time occupied by collisions can be ignored compared with the time between collisions.
4  The volume occupied by the molecules themselves can be ignored compared with the volume of the whole container.

**(b)** A gas consists of molecules which are bouncing off the walls of the container all the time.

At each collision, each molecule undergoes a change in momentum of $2\,mv$ ($m$ is its mass and $v$ is its average velocity).

This means a force acts on the molecule (Newton's Second Law) in the same direction as the change in momentum.

The force is equal to the change of momentum every second.

But Newton's Third Law states that if there is a force on the molecule, then there is an equal and opposite force on the wall.

Since there are many molecules bouncing off the walls every second, these will create a large total force.

If this force is divided by the area, this is equal to the pressure.

This is how a gas exerts pressure on the walls of the container.

**(c)** If the temperature increases, the average velocity of the molecules will increase and so will the change in momentum every second. If they move faster they will collide with the walls more often! Hence the pressure will increase.

**ANSWER**

**5**

**(a)** Ideal gas equation $PV = nRT$, where
$P$ is pressure of gas;
$V$ is volume of gas;
$n$ is number of moles;
$R$ is molar gas constant;
$T$ is temperature in Kelvin.

**(b)** $P_1 = 150$ kPa and $V_1 = 500$ cm$^3$
$P_2 = 200$ kPa and $V_2$ is unknown.
Since $T$ does not change, $P_1 V_1 = P_2 V_2$
$$150 \times 500 = 200 \times V_2 \qquad \therefore V_2 = 375\,\text{cm}^3.$$

**(c)** Heat will always be lost or gained from a system.

**(d)** This happens suddenly, so there is an adiabatic expansion.
The temperature will fall as the gas expands.

**6**

Boyle's Law states that the pressure of a gas is inversely proportional to the volume, provided the temperature remains constant.

Have you plotted the graph? Did you plot $P$ against $1/V$? This should be a straight line through the origin, since this shows that $P \propto 1/V$.

Have you done an experiment to show how the pressure of a gas varies with density?
Probably not! A bit of thinking required!
Have you done one to show how pressure varies with volume?
Since density = mass/volume, if mass is constant then density $\propto 1/\text{volume}$.
A graph of pressure against 1/volume should give the same relationship as pressure against density. So this is the graph you need to plot.
The conclusion is that the experiment required is one in which pressure and volume can be measured at constant temperature. You do not have to measure the density at all!
This experiment is given in all the textbooks. Look it up now.

## Section 2: Multiple Choice

**1**

**A** Since $P/T$ is constant at constant volume,
if original pressure, volume and temperature are $P$, $V$, $T$,

then final pressure, volume and temperature will be $\dfrac{P}{2}$, $V$, $\dfrac{T}{2}$.

The ideal gas equation gives
$PV = nRT$ where $n$ is number of moles and $R$ is molar gas constant.

Kinetic theory gives
$PV = \frac{1}{3}Nmc^2$
where $N$ is number of molecules, each of mass $m$ and $c^2$ is mean square velocity of the molecules.

For temperature $T$,  $nRT = \frac{1}{3}Nmc^2$           (1)

For temperature $\dfrac{T}{2}$,  $\dfrac{nRT}{2} = \frac{1}{3}Nmc_2{}^2$     (2)

where $c_2{}^2$ is mean square velocity of the molecules at the second temperature.

Divide (2) by (1)

$$\frac{T/2}{T} = \frac{c_2{}^2}{c^2}$$

$$\frac{1}{2} = \frac{c_2{}^2}{c^2}.$$

Take square root

$$\frac{c}{\sqrt{2}} = c_2.$$

**2**

**B** Each gas when mixed will behave as if the other gas is not there (Dalton's Law) and the final pressure is found by adding the individual pressures of gas X and gas Y.

Final volume for both gases = (6 + 2) = 8 litres

For gas X $\qquad P_1 V_1 = P_2 V_2$ (constant temperature)

$$(10 \times 10^4)(2) = (P_2)(8)$$
$$2.5 \times 10^4 \, \text{Pa} = P_2.$$

For gas Y $\qquad P_1 V_1 = P_2 V_2$

$$(2 \times 10^4)(6) = (P_2)(8)$$
$$1.5 \times 10^4 \, \text{Pa} = P_2.$$

Final pressure = $(2.5 \times 10^4 + 1.5 \times 10^4)$ Pa.

**3**

**A** The root mean square speed is a very important special average.
To calculate it you work the three steps backwards:
1 square  2 mean  3 root

1 square $\qquad 3^2 \quad 4^2 \quad 5^2 \quad 6^2 \quad 7^2$

2 take mean $\qquad \dfrac{3^2 + 4^2 + 5^2 + 6^2 + 7^2}{5}$

3 take root $\qquad \sqrt{\dfrac{(3^2 + 4^2 + 5^2 + 6^2 + 7^2)}{5}}$

$$= 5.2 \, \text{m s}^{-1}.$$

**4**

**E** If the mass of gas is fixed, the number of molecules cannot change!
At constant temperature the average velocity does not change either. Average momentum and kinetic energy will therefore remain constant. However, pressure is caused by the collisions of the molecules with the wall and the number of collisions per second is the important factor here.

**5**

**B** For gas A $\qquad$ Pressure $(P_A)$ = 16 atmospheres

Volume $(V_A)$ = 8 litres

Number of molecules $(n_A)$ = $4 \times 10^{23}$

Use $PV = nRT$: $\quad (16)(8) = (4 \times 10^{23}) T_A.$ (1)

For gas B $\qquad$ Pressure $(P_B)$ = 8 atmospheres

Volume $(V_B)$ = 4 litres

Number of molecules $(n_B)$ = $8 \times 10^{23}$

Use $PV = nRT$: $\quad (8)(4) = (8 \times 10^{23}) T_B.$ (2)

Divide equation (1) by equation (2)

$$\frac{(16)(8)}{(8)(4)} = \frac{(4 \times 10^{23})T_A}{(8 \times 10^{23})T_B}$$

$$8 = \frac{T_A}{T_B}.$$

**ANSWER**

**6**

**A**    Gas N    Volume   = 8 litres
                 Pressure = 24 kPa

      Gas M    Volume   = 4 litres
                 Pressure = 12 kPa

When the gases mix, each gas will spread out to fill the new volume (8 + 4 = 12 litres). Each gas exerts its own pressure. The resultant pressure will be the sum of these two new pressures.

For gas N          $P_1V_1 = P_2V_2$
                    $(24)(8) = P_2(12)$
                         $P_2 = 16$ kPa.

For gas M          $P_1'V_1' = P_2'V_2'$
                    $(12)(4) = P_2'(12)$
                         $P_2' = 4$ kPa.

So the resultant pressure = 16 + 4
                          = 20 kPa.

**7**

**B**  If $c$ is RMS speed at temperature $T$:
      From the kinetic theory      $T \propto c^2$ or $T = kc^2$
      At temperature $T'$           $T' \propto (2c)^2$ or $T' = k(2c)^2$

$$\frac{T'}{T} = \frac{k(2c)^2}{kc^2}$$

$$T' = \frac{4c^2}{c^2}T$$

If $T = 300$ K,   $T' = 4 \times 300$
                  = 1200 K.

**8**

**A**  QR is an isothermal expansion curve (D and E are wrong)
      RS is an adiabatic compression curve (B and C are wrong)
      The adiabatic curve has a steeper slope than the isothermal.

**ANSWER**

**9**

**B**  Are you familiar with this experiment?
You need to know it – look it up! Did you meet it in section 1 above?
You are observing the motion of smoke particles – they will move faster if the temperature rises. You cannot see the gas molecules. You can only see the effects they are causing.

**10**

**D**  The molar heat capacity is the amount of heat required to raise the temperature of one mole of gas through 1°C. If the gas is not allowed to expand (that is, the volume is kept constant) then no external work has to be done.
If the gas is allowed to expand (that is, the pressure is kept constant but the volume is allowed to change) then energy has to be used to do external work against the external pressure.

# Test 11

## Current electricity

### Section 1: Short Questions

**ANSWER**

**1**

**(a)**

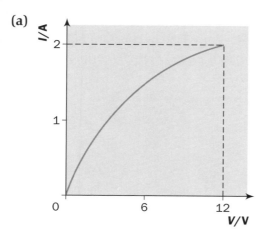

You must use the information you are given. A 12 V, 24 W lamp means that at operating voltage of 12 V the current $I$ can be found from

$I$ = power/p.d.
= 24/12
= 2 A.

Put any numbers you can on the graph.

**(b)** An electrical experiment requires a circuit diagram

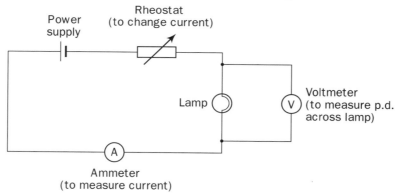

Remember nothing is obvious! You must give step-by-step instructions here:
1   Set up the above circuit.
2   Record p.d. across the lamp ($V$) using a voltmeter and current through the lamp ($I$) using an ammeter.
3   Vary the rheostat to give a range of values of ($V$) and ($I$);
4   Plot a graph of ($I$) against ($V$).
5   Check that your graph 'matches' the one above.

(c) The filament does not obey Ohm's Law.
  Ohm's Law states $I \propto V$ if physical conditions remain constant.
  The graph is not linear ($I$ is not directly proportional to $V$).
  The temperature of the filament is rising (physical conditions do not remain constant).

**ANSWER**

**2**

To derive $I = nAve$ (LEARN THE FOLLOWING!)

where $I$ is current flowing in a conductor;
  $n$ is number of 'free' electrons per unit volume;
  $A$ is cross-sectional area of the conductor;
  $v$ is drift velocity of free electrons;
  $e$ is charge on each electron.

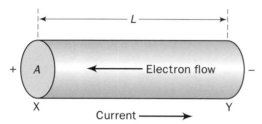

A current ($I$) is flowing due to the p.d. across the conductor.

$$\text{Volume of section XY} = AL$$
$$\text{Number of 'free' electrons in XY} = nAL$$
$$\text{Charge on these 'free' electrons in XY} = nALe.$$
$$\text{Since time} = \frac{\text{distance}}{\text{velocity}}$$

the time for all these electrons to leave area X $= \dfrac{L}{v}$

$$\text{Charge/second passing X} = \frac{\text{total charge}}{\text{time}}$$

$$= \frac{nALe}{L/v}$$

$$= nAve$$

But this is the current: so $\quad I = nAve$

Intrinsic semiconductor:
As the temperature rises, $n$ increases and from the formula above the current ($I$) increases.
For a constant p.d. the resistance ($R$) of the conductor will decrease and since
$R = \rho L/A$, the resistivity ($\rho$) will also decrease.

(a) Measure $V$ on voltmeter (p.d. across R).
Measure $I$ on ammeter (current through R).
Vary R and repeat to get a set of values of $V$ and $I$.

(b) Plot $V$ against $I$.
Since $V = E - Ir$,     $(y = c + mx)$

a graph of $V$ against $I$ will be linear:

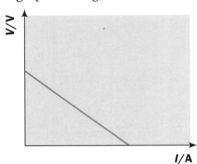

(c) To find $E$: measure $y$ intercept;
$\quad\quad\quad\quad y$ intercept $= E$
To find $r$: measure slope $m$ (slope is negative).
Slope $= -r$ ($r$ is positive).

**4**

(a) The oscilloscope measures the p.d. across R.

Since $V = IR$ and $R$ is constant,
$\quad V \propto I$

(i) If $S_1$ is closed, the current in R will be an alternating current.

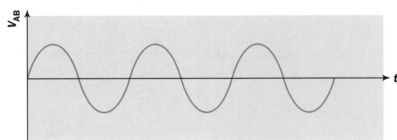

(ii) If $S_1$ is open, then the diode will only allow current to flow one way.

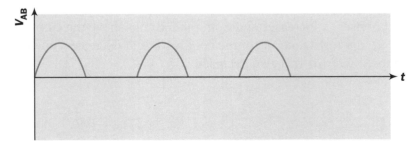

**(b)** Alternating current – the electrons oscillate about a mean position as the p.d. changes from positive to negative.
Direct current – the electrons move in the same direction all the time, i.e. towards the positive potential.

**(c)** 240 $V_{rms}$    For 60 W lamp,

$$\text{Average power} = V_{rms} \times I_{rms}$$
$$60 = 240 \times I_{rms}$$
$$0.25 \text{ A} = I_{rms}$$

The peak current ($I_0$)    $I_0 = I_{rms} \times \sqrt{2} = 0.35$ A.

**ANSWER**

**5**

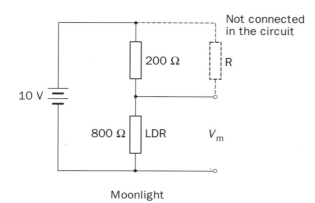

Moonlight

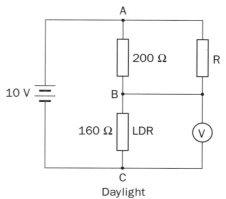

Daylight

Consider circuit in moonlight (switch open).
By potential divider

$$V_m = \frac{800}{(800 + 200)} \times 10$$

$$= 8 \text{ V}$$

Consider circuit in daylight (switch closed).

   (*V*) reads 8 V

Let total resistance between A and B (200 and *R* in parallel)

   $= R^*$

By potential divider p.d. across BC = 8 V

$$8 = \left(\frac{160}{160 + R^*}\right) \times 10$$
$$R^* = 40 \text{ } \Omega$$

Total resistance between A and B = 40 $\Omega$

Therefore $\dfrac{1}{40} = \dfrac{1}{200} + \dfrac{1}{R}$

$R = 50 \text{ } \Omega$.

(a) Resistance = $\dfrac{\text{potential difference across a conductor}}{\text{current through conductor}}$

(b) For the metal conductor:

From graph $\quad R = \dfrac{V}{I}$

$$= \dfrac{5}{8 \times 10^{-3}}$$

$$= 625\ \Omega.$$

(c) Non-ohmic conductor does not obey Ohm's Law.
Graph of $V$ against $I$ will not be a straight line, e.g. thermistor.

Resistivity $\rho$ can be calculated from $R = \rho L/A$.
$R$ is resistance of the nichrome wire, $L$ its length and $A$ its cross-sectional area.
If $L$ is measured using a metre rule, $d$ diameter measured using micrometer,
$R$ found from an electrical experiment, then $\rho$ can be calculated from:
$\rho = AR/L$ where $A = \pi d^2/4$
The electrical experiment could use the following circuit.

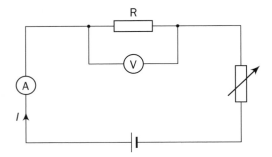

For a range of readings of the rheostat, record $V$ using voltmeter and $I$ using ammeter.
Plot a graph of $V$ against $I$ and measure the slope (slope = $R$). Substitute into above
equation to find $\rho$.

## Section 2: Multiple Choice

ANSWER

1

E

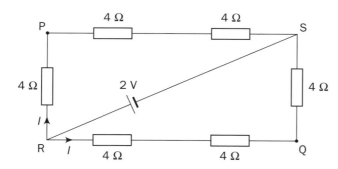

For top branch RPS

    Potential drop across RS = 2 V

    Potential drop across RP = $IR$

$$= \left(\frac{2}{12}\right)4$$

$$= \frac{2}{3} \text{ V}$$

Potential at P = 2 – 2/3     = $1\frac{1}{3}$ V

For lower branch RQS

    Potential drop across RS = 2 V

    Potential drop across RQ = $IR$

$$= \left(\frac{2}{12}\right)8$$

$$= 1\frac{1}{3} \text{ V}$$

Potential at Q = 2 – $1\frac{1}{3}$ = $\frac{2}{3}$ V

So potential at P is higher than the potential at Q.

    Difference in potential    = $1\frac{1}{3} - \frac{2}{3}$

                                   = $\frac{2}{3}$ V.

2

C   When Y is on the left hand side of the 4 Ω resistor, the potential difference (p.d.) across XY will be zero. When Y is on the right hand side of the 4 Ω resistor, the p.d. will be equal to the p.d. across the 4 Ω resistor.

Use the formula $E = I(r + R)$.

To find the p.d. across the 4 Ω resistor, remember the internal resistance ($r$) of the battery will reduce the current.

# Test 11

Potential difference across 4 Ω resistor $= IR$

$$= \left(\frac{E}{r + R}\right)R$$

$$= \left(\frac{4}{2 + 4}\right)4$$

$$= 2\tfrac{2}{3}\text{V}.$$

ANSWER

**3**

**D** Since point M is earthed, M at zero potential – a different arrangement from normal.

Potential difference across 6 Ω resistor $= IR$

$$= \left(\frac{E}{r + R}\right)R$$

$$= \left(\frac{12}{2 + 8}\right)6$$

$$= 7.2 \text{ V}.$$

So N must be 7.2 V higher than M.

**4**

**B** The heater rated 36 W, 12 V takes current 3 A so its resistance ($R$) is given by:

$$R = \frac{V}{I} = \frac{12}{3} = 4 \ \Omega$$

But $R = \rho \dfrac{L}{A}$ where $\rho$ is resistivity;

$L$ is length;

$A$ is area of cross section.

$L = AR/\rho$

$$= \frac{(0.5 \times 10^{-6})(4)}{2.5 \times 10^{-7}}$$

$$= 8.0 \text{ m}.$$

**5**

**C**

50 mA is too much current to go through the meter.
46 mA must be diverted through resistor R.
R is placed in parallel with the meter.
$R$ will be much smaller than 25 Ω.

The p.d. across XY $= (4.0 \times 10^{-3})(25)$

or p.d. across XY $= IR$

$$= (46 \times 10^{-3})(R)$$

$$(46 \times 10^{-3})(R) = (4.0 \times 10^{-3})(25)$$

$$R = 2.17\ \Omega.$$

**ANSWER**

**6**

**C**

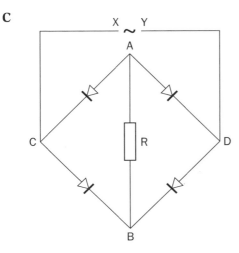

The alternating supply causes the potential at X continually to change from positive to negative. During the half of the cycle when X is positive, current flows along the path XCBADY. During the half of the cycle when X is negative, current flows along the path YDBACX, i.e. in R current always flows from B to A but will vary in magnitude.

**7**

**A** The p.d. across CD is that of the supply.

**8**

**B**

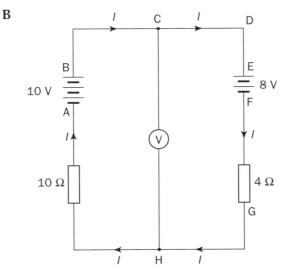

The batteries are in opposition. The resultant e.m.f. is 2 V. This e.m.f. will drive a current ($I$) clockwise around the circuit.

Total e.m.f.      =  2 V
Total resistance  =  10 + 4
                  =  14 $\Omega$

$$I = \frac{2}{14} = 0.143 \text{ A}.$$

Potential difference across AB = 10 V
Potential at B (and C) = 10 V

Current flows through the 8 V battery from E to F

Potential at E = 10 V
So potential at F = (10 – 8) = 2 V
Potential differences across FG = $I \times 4$
                    = (0.143)4 = 0.572 V
Potential at G = 2 – 0.572
              = 1.428 V
Potential at H = 1.428 V
Potential difference across CH = 10 – 1.428
                    = 8.6 V approximately.

**ANSWER**

**9**

**E**   Use   $R = \rho \dfrac{L}{A}$

$$= \rho \frac{L}{\pi d^2/4}$$

where  $\rho$ = resistivity
$L$ = length
$d$ = diameter
$A$ = cross-sectional area.

But  $\dfrac{\rho_P}{\rho_Q} = \dfrac{1}{2}$  and  $\dfrac{d_P}{d_Q} = \dfrac{1}{2}$  and  $\dfrac{L_P}{L_Q} = \dfrac{1}{2}$

So  $\dfrac{R_P}{R_Q} = \dfrac{4\rho_P L_P}{\pi d_P^2} \Big/ \dfrac{4\rho_Q L_Q}{\pi d_Q^2}$

$$= \left(\frac{\rho_P}{\rho_Q}\right)\left(\frac{L_P}{L_Q}\right)\left(\frac{d_Q^2}{d_P^2}\right)$$

$$= \left(\frac{1}{2}\right)\left(\frac{1}{2}\right)\left(\frac{4}{1}\right)$$

$$= 1.$$

**B** Normal rating of lamp 12 V, 24 W means the current is 2 A and the resistance 6 Ω. When connected to a 10 V supply the current will no longer be 2 A and the power will not be 24 W. The resistance will probably decrease slightly as well (metal filament).

To obtain an approximate value for the current ($I$), assume resistance ($R$) is about 6 Ω.

$$I = \frac{V}{R} = \frac{10}{6} = 1.67 \text{ A.}$$

# Test 12

## Magnetic effects of electricity

### Section 1: Short Questions

**ANSWER 1**

$$F = \frac{\mu_0 I_1 I_2}{2\pi r}$$

$$F \propto \frac{1}{r} \quad (\mu_0, I_1, I_2 \text{ constant})$$

To get a straight line graph:

$$F = \frac{\mu_0 I_1 I_2}{2\pi} \times \frac{1}{r}$$

$$Y = mx + c$$

is an equation of a straight line:

Plot $F$ against $1/r$

Slope of graph $(m)$:

$$m = \frac{\mu_0 I_1 I_2}{2\pi}$$

$$\therefore \mu_0 = \frac{2\pi m}{I_1 I_2}$$

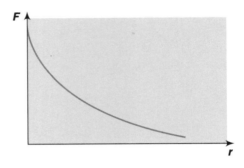

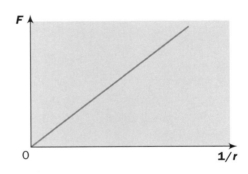

Hence to calculate $\mu_0$ measure slope $(m)$ and calculate from above equation.

**2**

**(a)**

Vertical wires

Horizontal plane

$F$ ← Electromagnetic force

Resultant B field

$F$ → Electromagnetic force

Draw the diagram very carefully. The labelled forces $F$ must show points of action (i.e. in contact with the wires).

# Test 12

**(b)** From the definition of the ampère

$$I_1 = I_2 = 1 \text{ ampère}$$
$$\text{Force/length} = 2 \times 10^{-7} \text{ N m}^{-1}$$
$$\text{Distance apart} = 1 \text{ metre}$$

Given formula

$$\frac{F}{L} = \frac{\mu_0 I_1 I_2}{2\pi r}$$

$$2 \times 10^{-7} = \frac{\mu_0 (1)(1)}{2\pi(1)}$$

$$\mu_0 = 4\pi \times 10^{-7}.$$

To find units of $\mu_0$

$$\mu_0 = \frac{F(2\pi r)}{L(I_1)(I_2)} = \frac{(N)(m)}{(m)(A)(A)} = N\,A^{-2}.$$

**ANSWER**

**3**

**(a)** Read the question carefully. It is about electromagnetic induction and ENERGY. We can trace the stages step by step.

1 Electrical energy is supplied to coil A.
2 The current in A produces a magnetic field so magnetic energy is stored around A.
3 The magnetic field around A also links coil B.
4 Since the magnetic field is changing (owing to alternating current) electrical energy is produced in coil B by laws of electromagnetic induction.
5 The electrical energy in B is dissipated as heat and light in the lamp.

**(b)** The iron bar increases the flux linkage between the two coils, so the energy transfer is more efficient.
The e.m.f. induced in B is increased, causing increased current. The lamp will brighten.

**4**

**(a)** Force exerted on the wire by the magnetic field

$$F = BIL = (50 \times 10^{-3})(0.5)(51 \times 10^{-3})$$
$$= 1.3 \times 10^{-3} \text{ N}.$$

To find $I$ use amps $\times$ volts $=$ watts
$I \times 6 = 3$
$I = 0.5$ A.

_A-Level Physics: Structured Questions & Multiple Choice_ **157**

**(b)** By the left hand rule (Fleming's) force on wire is UP. If the magnetic field is reversed force on wire is DOWN.

Original reading = 153.860 g.

Force due to magnetic field is UP so reading is too small so extra mass needs to be added.

Force due to magnetic field   = $1.3 \times 10^{-3}$ N from above

Effective mass due to field   = $\dfrac{1.3 \times 10^{-3}}{9.8} = 1.3 \times 10^{-4}$ kg

Hence true effective mass before the field is reversed
= (153.860 + 0.13) g

When the force is down (field reversed)
New effective mass       = 153.860 + 0.13 + 0.13
= $154.12 \times 10^{-3}$ kg.

**ANSWER**

**5**

The diagram required is as shown.
Remember to explain your symbols.

To calculate **(c)** use the formula
$B = \mu_0 I / 2\pi d$
$= 4\pi \times 10^{-7} \times 1000 / 2\pi \times 20 \times 10^{-2}$
$= 1 \times 10^{-3}$ T.

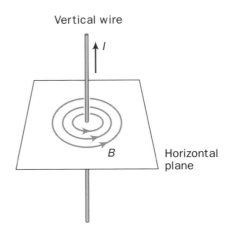

**6**

**(a)** There are two laws of electromagnetic induction.
Faraday's Law states that when there is relative motion between a magnetic field and a conductor, an e.m.f. $E$ is induced in the conductor where $E$ is proportional to the rate of change of flux linkage. Lenz's Law states that the direction of $E$ always tries to oppose the change causing it.

**(b)** An e.m.f. is induced in the coil, due to the moving magnet. The magnet causes a changing magnetic flux to link the turns of the coil. Faraday's Law says an e.m.f. will be induced in the conductor (the coil).

**(c)** By Lenz's Law, as the magnet falls towards X, a north pole will tend to be induced at X (and a south at Y). As the magnet leaves Y, a north pole will tend to be induced at Y (and a south at X). So the situation changes halfway through the process (at Z).
The induced e.m.f. will change direction as the magnet passes through Z. The induced e.m.f. will be a minimum at Z. The induced e.m.f. will be very small when the magnet is a long way away from the coil. The graph will look like this.

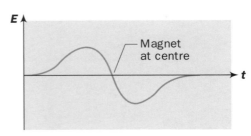

The tesla is defined by the following formula: $F = BIL$.
In words, the magnetic flux density of a magnetic field is one tesla if the force on a wire (1 m long and carrying current of 1 A) sitting in that field is 1 N. As a word equation:

tesla = newtons/ampères × metres

**(a)** To find $B$ we need to know the current through the coil.
For this circuit $E = 1.5$ V
Total resistance $= 0.2 + 0.4 = 0.6 \, \Omega$
∴ Current $= 1.5/0.6 = 2.5$ A
For solenoid at centre, $B = \mu_0 N I/L$
$= 4\pi \times 10^{-7} \times 1000 \times 2.5/50 \times 10^{-2} = 200\pi \times 10^{-5}$ T.

**(b)** Magnetic flux $= A\,B = 1.0 \times 10^{-2} \times 200\pi \times 10^{-5} = 200\pi \times 10^{-7}$ Wb.

# Section 2: Multiple Choice

**1**

**A** If $E$ is induced e.m.f., $B$ magnetic flux density, $L$ and $v$ are respectively the length and speed of the axle.

Use $E = BLv$
$= (4 \times 10^{-5})(1.4)(15)$
$= 84 \times 10^{-5}$
$= 8.4 \times 10^{-4}$ V.

**2**

**E** This question is about eddy currents — currents that swirl around in blocks of metallic material, due to induced e.m.f.s caused when the metal cuts a magnetic field (Faraday's Law of Electromagnetic Induction). Induced e.m.f.s will occur in both P and Q, since they are both made of metal.

However, it is the induced *current* (eddy current) which causes an induced magnetic field — and this induced field opposes that caused by the horseshoe magnet, slowing P and Q down. The induced current will be larger in P (its resistance is less) so the effect is more noticeable in P. P slows down first.

**3**

**D** Faraday's Law of Electromagnetic Induction applies here, i.e. induced e.m.f. ($E$) is proportional to the rate of change of flux linkage. Any quantity that increases the flux linkage will increase the e.m.f. between XY. Answers A, B, C and E all decrease the flux linkage. A laminated core will reduce energy losses by reducing eddy currents, so there will be more energy available. The e.m.f. across XY will increase.

**ANSWER**

**4**

**A**    Force/unit length $= \dfrac{\mu I_1 I_2}{2\pi d}$

$$I_1 = 2.0 \text{ A}$$
$$I_2 = 1.5 \text{ A}$$
$$\mu_0 = 4\pi \times 10^{-7} \text{ H m}^{-1}$$
$$d = 20 \times 10^{-2} \text{ m}$$

Force/unit length $= \dfrac{(4\pi \times 10^{-7})(2.0)(1.5)}{(2)\pi(20 \times 10^{-2})}$

$$= 3.0 \times 10^{-6} \text{ N m}^{-1}.$$

The force on both wires is the same.

**5**

**D**    The wire will experience a force according to Fleming's left hand rule.

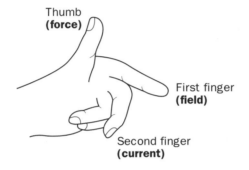

Thumb **(force)**

First finger **(field)**

Second finger **(current)**

**6**

**E**    Since a conductor (the metal disc) is cutting magnetic lines of flux, an e.m.f. ($E$) will be induced according to Faraday's Law of Electromagnetic Induction,

where $E = \dfrac{d\Phi}{dt}$

and $\Phi =$ magnetic flux
$\Phi =$ (area cut)(magnetic flux density)
$t =$ time in seconds.

Increasing the rate of change of flux linkage will increase the e.m.f. Answers B, C and D are all correct. The e.m.f. across QR is equal to the e.m.f. across PQ but there will be no resultant e.m.f. across PR.

**7**

**C**    P will exert a force on Q. Q will exert an equal but opposite force on P. This is Newton's THIRD Law.

ANSWER

**8**

**B** At the neutral point (where there is zero resultant flux density) the uniform magnetic flux ($2.0 \times 10^{-5}$ T) is equal to the flux created by the current-carrying wire.

For a long straight wire in air:

Magnetic flux density $= \dfrac{\mu_0 I}{2\pi d}$

$$2.0 \times 10^{-5} = \frac{(4\pi \times 10^{-7})(I)}{2\pi \times 0.15}$$

$$15 \text{ A} = I.$$

**9**

**E** For solenoid field at centre $B = \mu_0 N I / L$
$= 4\pi \times 10^{-7} \times 400 \times 2.0/50 \times 10^{-2}$
$= 2.0 \times 10^{-3}$ T.

**10**

**D** Apply Faraday's Law here. If you increase the rate of flux linkage in any way, you will increase the e.m.f.:

A   Does not affect the e.m.f. – it would affect the current.
B   Is much the same as A.
C   Would make flux linkage smaller, not bigger.
D   Will increase the rate and therefore the e.m.f.
E   Must be wrong if D is correct! What effect would this have?

# Test 13

## Electric and gravitational fields

### Section 1: Short Questions

**ANSWER**

**1**

(a) Gravitational field is a region in which gravitational forces act on masses.

(b) Gravitational field strength is the force acting on one kilogram at a certain point in the field. For a satellite following a circular path:

$$\frac{mv^2}{r} = \frac{GmM}{r^2}$$

$$v^2 = \frac{GM}{r}$$

But $v^2 = \frac{4\pi^2 r^2}{T^2}$

$$\frac{GM}{r} = \frac{4\pi^2 r^2}{T^2}$$

where $m$ is mass of satellite;
$M$ is mass of earth;
$v$ is velocity of satellite;
$r$ is radius of orbit;
$G$ is universal constant of gravitation;
$T$ is time period of satellite.

Rearrange to get required formula!

**2**

(a) G is the universal constant in the equation

$$F = G\frac{m_1 m_2}{d^2}$$

If $m_1 = m_2 = 1$ kg, and $d = 1$ metre then $G = F$
or, if two masses are placed 1 metre apart, then the force between them is equal to $G$ (magnitude $6.7 \times 10^{-11}$ N m$^2$ kg$^{-2}$).

(b) $G$ is the universal constant given above, but $g$ is acceleration due to gravity on the surface of the earth.

(c) Look up this experiment in your textbook. Various physical principles are involved. Two tiny masses are attached, one to each end of a light rod. Each is attracted to a large mass such that the rod rotates through a small angle until the torque exerted by the rod is balanced by the gravitational forces. By measuring the forces, distances and masses, $G$ can be found.

**ANSWER**

**3**

This law states that the force between two masses is directly proportional to the product of the masses and inversely proportional to the square of their distance apart.

**(a)** Weight = mass × g' where g' is acceleration due to gravity in the orbit (not 9.8 m s⁻²)

$$= GmM/r^2$$
$$= (6.67 \times 10^{-11})(100)(6.0 \times 10^{24})/(1.0 \times 10^9)^2$$
$$= 40.0 \times 10^{-3} \text{ N.}$$

**(b)** Gravitational P.E. $= mgh = 100 \times \dfrac{4.0 \times 10^{-3}\text{N}}{100} \times 1000 = 40.0$ J.

**(c)** This is an approximation, since g is not constant.

**4**

Electric field strength is the force per unit charge acting at a point. It is measured in $NC^{-1}$. The following diagrams show the field lines.

**(a)**

**(b)**

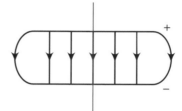

**5**

$F = kr^{-2}$

**(a)**

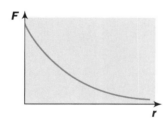

**(b)**

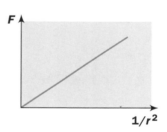

$F \propto kr^{-2}$    Examples are:  1  force between two masses;  2  force between two charges.

**6**

**(a)** 28 days approximately.

**(b)**

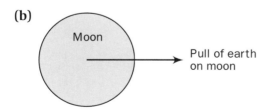

**(c)** If body A exerts a force on body B, then body B exerts a force on body A. These forces are equal but in opposite directions along the same line.

**(d)** The moon pulls on the earth and the earth pulls on the moon. These forces are equal to one another but in opposite directions. This is Newton's Third Law.

**7**

(a) $F = \dfrac{1}{4\pi\varepsilon}\dfrac{q_1 q_2}{r^2} = \dfrac{1}{4\pi\varepsilon}\dfrac{2 \times 10^{-9} \times 2 \times 10^{-9}}{(10^{-2})^2} = 3.6 \times 10^{-4}$ N.

If the force is given then do the calculation in reverse, remembering to take the square root to find the distance. The answer is 6.0 cm.

(b) Use the formula:

$$\tfrac{1}{2}mv^2 = Ve$$

$$\therefore v^2 = \frac{2eV}{m}$$

$$\therefore v^2 = \frac{2(1.6 \times 10^{-19})(600)}{9 \times 10^{-31}}$$

$$= 213 \times 10^{12}$$

$$v = 14.6 \times 10^6 \text{ m s}^{-1}.$$

# Section 2: Multiple Choice

**1**

**E** Alpha ($\alpha$) particles are helium nuclei. Each alpha particle contains two protons and two neutrons. Each alpha particle has a positive charge and will be deflected in electric *and* magnetic fields. Alpha particles have a very small range in air and cannot travel through metal.

**2**

**C** This is Newton's Third Law. The two forces are equal.

**3**

**D**

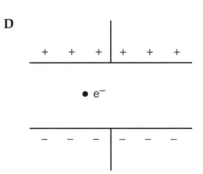

A uniform electric field is created by using two charged plates. The stationary electron will be subjected to a force pulling it towards the positively charged plate. The electron will travel in a straight line.

**4**

**E** Force $F = \dfrac{1}{4\pi\varepsilon}\dfrac{q_1 q_2}{r^2}$ where $\varepsilon$ is permittivity.

**ANSWER**

**5**

A

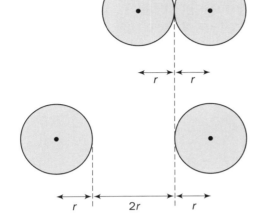

Distance between centres = 2r

$$F = \frac{G(m)(m)}{(2r)^2}$$

$$F = \frac{Gm^2}{4r^2}.$$

Distance between centres = 4r

$$F' = \frac{G(m)(m)}{(4r)^2}$$

$$F' = \frac{Gm^2}{16r^2}.$$

The new gravitational attraction when one sphere is moved away through a distance of 2r is one quarter of the original.

**6**

**B** This is Coulomb's Law. Learn it!

**7**

A Gravitational force = mass × acceleration

= (100)(5)

= 500 N.

(Gravitational field strength of 5 N kg$^{-1}$ will produce an acceleration of 5 m s$^{-2}$ on a mass of 1 kg.)

**8**

**B** Since both particles are stationary, the forces on them are balanced.

For P $\quad mg = \dfrac{V}{d}q_P$ (1)

For Q $\quad 3mg = \dfrac{V}{d}q_Q$ (2)

Divide (2) by (1)

$$3 = \frac{q_Q}{q_P}.$$

The charge on Q is three times that on P. When the plates move further apart the electric force on both decreases. The weights are now larger than the electric forces and both P and Q will accelerate DOWN. Since P has the smaller mass it will have the larger acceleration.

**D**  For a satellite following a circular path:

$$\frac{mv^2}{r} = \frac{GmM}{r^2}$$

$$v^2 = \frac{GM}{r}$$

But  $v^2 = \frac{4\pi^2 r^2}{T^2}$

where $m$ is mass of satellite;
$M$ is mass of the planet;
$v$ is velocity of satellite;
$r$ is radius of orbit;
$G$ is universal constant of gravitation;
$T$ is time period of satellite.

$$\frac{GM}{r} = \frac{4\pi^2 r^2}{T^2}$$

Now we introduce density $\Delta$ = mass/volume

$$= M / \frac{4}{3}\pi R^3 \qquad \text{where } R \text{ is radius of the planet}$$

$$\therefore M = \frac{4}{3}\pi R^3 \Delta.$$

Substitute for $M$ in the above equation and rearrange to get $T^2\Delta$.

**10**

**B**  Electric field intensity is force per unit charge, but can be calculated from

$E = V/d$     where $V$ is p.d. across the plates;
               $d$ is distance between plates.

$E \propto 1/d$ or $E \propto d^{-1}$ or here $x \propto y^{-1}$.

# Test 14

## Capacitors

## Section 1: Short Questions

**ANSWER 1**

Note the quantities on the axes (and the units!).
Charge ($Q$) in microcoulombs
Time ($t$) in milliseconds
For S.I. system you must use coulombs and seconds.
Slope of graph $= \Delta Q/\Delta t$
$\qquad\qquad$ = rate of change of charge with time
$\qquad\qquad$ = current.

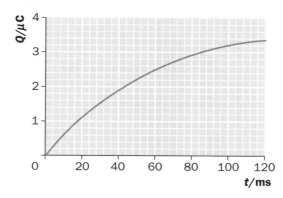

The average current is found by measuring the slope of the line AB.
Complete the triangle carefully (make it large).

$$\text{Average current} = \frac{(3.2 - 1.9)10^{-6}\ \text{C}}{(100 - 40)10^{-3}\ \text{s}}$$

$$= 22 \times 10^{-6}\ \text{A} \quad = 22\ \mu\text{A}.$$

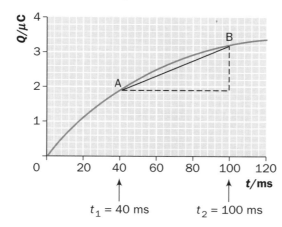

$t_1 = 40$ ms $\qquad$ $t_2 = 100$ ms

The instantaneous current is found by drawing a tangent CD at time $t$ = 40 ms.
Measure the slope of the tangent.

$$\text{Instantaneous current} = \frac{(3.3 - 0.7)10^{-6} \text{ C}}{(80 - 0)10^{-3} \text{ s}}$$

$$= 32 \times 10^{-6} \text{ A} \quad = 32 \text{ } \mu\text{A}.$$

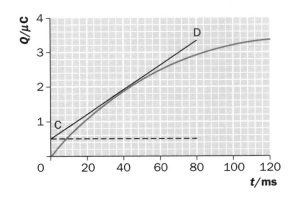

The graph used to find the average current uses the two times shown ($t_1$ = 40 ms
and $t_2$ = 100 ms).
As the time interval becomes shorter, the points A and B get closer and closer until they
coincide, i.e average current → instantaneous current.

**ANSWER**

**2**

$$\text{Time constant} = RC$$
$$= (0.4 \times 10^{6})(3 \times 10^{-6})$$
$$= 1.2 \text{ s}$$

$$V = V_0 e^{-\frac{1}{RC}t}$$

$$\ln V = \ln V_0 - \frac{1}{RC}t \quad \therefore \ln(2.94) = \ln(8.00) - \frac{1}{1.2}t$$

$$1.08 = 2.08 - \frac{1}{1.2}t \quad \therefore t = (2.08 - 1.08)(1.2) = 1.2 \text{ s}.$$

If the value of $R$ is 2 MΩ the time constant will be larger and the capacitor take longer to
discharge.

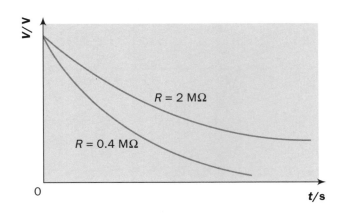

At discharge, electrons flow via R from the top plate to the bottom plate. If the resistance is increased, the electrons find it harder to follow this path so the process takes longer.

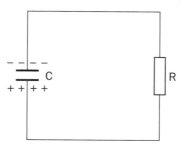

**ANSWER**

**3**

(a) Energy stored $= \frac{1}{2}CV^2 = \frac{1}{2}(72 \times 10^{-12})(12)^2 = 5.2 \times 10^{-9}$ J.

(b) Charge constant; distance between plates increased so the capacitance ($C = \varepsilon A/d$) decreases and p.d. increases ($V = Q/C$).

Original $Q = VC = (12)(72 \times 10^{-12}) = 864 \times 10^{-12}$ C.

Since distance between plates is doubled capacitance is halved.

New capacitance $= 36$ pF

Energy stored $= \frac{1}{2}Q^2/C = \frac{1}{2}(864 \times 10^{-12})^2/(36 \times 10^{-12})$
$= 10.4 \times 10^{-9}$ J

Answer in (b) is larger because work has been added by separating the charged plates.

$$\text{Average force} = \frac{\text{work done}}{\text{distance}} = \frac{(10.4 - 5.2)10^{-9}}{5 \times 10^{-3}}$$

$$= 1.04 \times 10^{-6} \text{ N.}$$

**4**

(a) Time constant $= RC$
$= (200 \times 10^3)(2000 \times 10^{-6})$
$= 400$ s

(b)

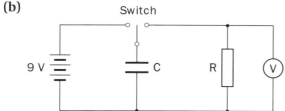

(c) 1  Connect C to supply to charge up capacitor.
2  Connect C to R to discharge capacitor.
3  During discharge record voltmeter reading ($V$) at suitable time intervals ($t$). Remember $RC = 400$ s.
4  Plot graph $V$ against $t$.

**(a)** Energy stored $= \frac{1}{2}CV^2$ (look up proof).

**(b)** Energy stored $= \frac{1}{2}(3 \times 10^{-6})(20)^2$
$= 6.0 \times 10^{-4}$ J.

**(c)**

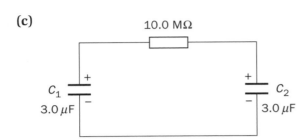

These capacitors are in a series circuit, but plates with similar charges are connected together and once current ceases to flow, the p.d. across them will be the same.

Total capacitance $= C_1 + C_2 = 6.0 \times 10^{-6}$ F

Total charge $Q_2 =$ initial charge on $C_1$

$$Q_2 = Q_1 = C_1 V_1$$
$$= (3.0 \times 10^{-6})(20)$$
$$= 6.0 \times 10^{-5} \text{ C}$$

Final potential for both $= \dfrac{\text{total charge}}{\text{total capacitance}}$

$$= 6.0 \times 10^{-5}/6.0 \times 10^{-6}$$
$$= 10 \text{ V}$$

Final energy stored on both $= (\frac{1}{2})(6.0 \times 10^{-6})(10)^2$
$= 3.0 \times 10^{-4}$ J

Energy dissipated in resistor $=$ Initial energy – final energy
$= 3.0 \times 10^{-4}$ J.

**(d)** Energy dissipated is the difference between initial and final energies stored by the two capacitors. The magnitude of the resistor affects the time the process takes, but not the amount of energy dissipated.

**(a)** Capacitance is defined by: $\dfrac{\text{the charge stored on one plate of the capacitor}}{\text{p.d. across the plates}}$

**(b)** When the switch S is closed, electrons move from plate X to plate Y, using the energy from the battery.

**(c)** An alternating source means the electrons will oscillate about a mean position, rather than flowing in one direction.

**ANSWER**

**7**

Since the relationship to be investigated is $C = \varepsilon A/d$ you need a circuit which will measure capacitance. You also need to be able to change the area of overlap of the plates $A$ and the separation $d$.

Two experiments are required:
1 Variation of $C$ with $A$.
2 Variation of $C$ with $d$.

Experiment (1). Use the circuit below to measure capacitance.

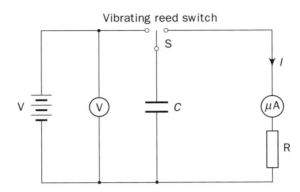

Vibrating reed switch

S is a reed switch, which alternately charges and discharges the capacitor $C$.
Record current $I$ using the microammeter. Knowing $n$, the frequency of the reed switch, calculate $C$ using the formula $I = nCV$.
Change area of overlap of plates to get a range of values for $C$ and $A$, keeping $d$ same. Plot a graph of $C$ against $A$.

Experiment (2). Use the same circuit, but this time record $C$ for different values of $d$ keeping $A$ constant. Which graph should you plot this time?

## Section 2: Multiple Choice

**1**

**B**   For capacitors $C_1$ and $C_2$ in series giving total capacitance $C_T$

$$\frac{1}{C_T} = \frac{1}{C_1} + \frac{1}{C_2}$$

so $$\frac{1}{2} = \frac{1}{C} + \frac{1}{C}$$

$$\frac{1}{2} = \frac{2}{C}$$

$$C = 4 \ \mu F.$$

For capacitors in parallel

$$C_T = C_1 + C_2$$

so $$C_T = 4 + 4$$
$$= 8 \ \mu F.$$

**2**

**C** If $Q$ is the charge on the capacitor of capacitance $C$;
$V$ is the p.d. across its plates;
$\varepsilon$ is permittivity of the medium between the plates;
$A$ is area of overlap of the plates;
$d$ is distance between the plates;

then $Q = VC$ and $C = \dfrac{\varepsilon A}{d}$

$$Q = \frac{V(\varepsilon A)}{d}$$

$$Q \propto 1/d$$

i.e. when $d$ is small $Q$ is large and when $d$ is large $Q$ is small.

**3**

**D** The 9.0 $\mu$F capacitor connected to 200 V source receives charge $Q$ where:

$Q = VC$
$Q = (200)(9.0 \times 10^{-6})$ C
$\quad = 1800 \times 10^{-6}$ C

The two capacitors in parallel create a total capacitance of $(9.0 + 3.0) = 12$ $\mu$F

The charge on these $\quad = 1800 \times 10^{-6}$ C

p.d. across them $\quad V_T = \dfrac{1800 \times 10^{-6}}{12 \times 10^{-6}}$

$$= 150 \text{ V.}$$

**4**

**D** The charge ($Q$) on each capacitor is the same. The total capacitance ($C_T$) is given by

$$\frac{1}{C_T} = \frac{1}{C_1} + \frac{1}{C_2} + \frac{1}{C_3}$$

$$= \frac{1}{1} + \frac{1}{1} + \frac{1}{1}$$

$$C_T = \frac{1}{3} \; \mu F$$

But $Q = VC$
$\quad Q = (2)(\frac{1}{3} \times 10^{-6})$

$\quad\quad = \frac{2}{3} \times 10^{-6}$ C.

This is the total charge stored, but it is also the magnitude of charge stored on each capacitor.

**ANSWER**

**5**

**A** For a capacitor (capacitance $C$) connected to a source (potential difference $V$).
Charge $Q = VC$
If the capacitor is charged $n$ times/second

Charge received per second $\dfrac{Q}{t} = nVC$

But charge/second = current $I$

$I = nVC$
$\quad = (100)(10)(6 \times 10^{-4} \times 10^{-6})$
$\quad = 0.6 \times 10^{-6}$ A.

**6**

**A** Since the plates are connected to the battery all the time, the potential difference $V$ across the plates will not change. Plate Y is moved away so the capacitance $C$ must decrease.
Charge $(Q) = VC$ so if $C\downarrow Q\uparrow$
If charge moves in the circuit, energy is used. This energy probably comes from the battery.

Energy stored $(E)$ by the capacitor $= \frac{1}{2}CV^2$

If $C\downarrow E\downarrow$.

**7**

**C** Perhaps the easiest way to tackle this one is to assign values to the two capacitors. Let us take each capacitor as 2 $\mu$F. The total capacitance $(C_T)$ between X and Y will be:

$$\frac{1}{C_T} = \frac{1}{2} + \frac{1}{2} \quad \therefore C_T = 1 \ \mu F$$

Consider each suggestion in turn, remembering capacitance $C = \dfrac{\varepsilon A}{d}$.

A  In parallel the total capacitance

$$= 2 + 2 \quad = 4 \ \mu F.$$

B  A dielectric material will increase both capacitance, say, to 3 $\mu$F each:

Total capacitance $= \dfrac{1}{1/3 + 1/3} = \dfrac{3}{2} \ \mu F$, i.e. larger.

C  Doubling the plate separation of one capacitor will decrease its value to 1 $\mu$F:

Total capacitance $= \dfrac{1}{1/2 + 1/1} = \dfrac{2}{3} \ \mu F$, i.e. smaller.

D  Halving the plate separation of both:

Total capacitance $= \dfrac{1}{1/4 + 1/4} = 2 \ \mu F$, i.e. larger.

E  Shorting out one capacitor will give total capacitance between X and Y = 2 $\mu$F, i.e. larger.

**8**

**A** Since the capacitor is connected to the battery all the time, the p.d. across it will not change. Look at the formula for capacitance. You will see that capacitance must change. ($C = \varepsilon A/d$) so charge on each plate will change and so will the energy stored.

**9**

**B** Call each capacitor $C$, and calculate each circuit in turn.

A – Capacitance = $C/4$ (these are in series so use $1/C_T = 1/C_1 + 1/C_2 +$ etc.).

B – For lowest branch only $C/2$ then add $C + C = 5C/2$.

C – Top branch = $C/2$ and bottom branch = $C/2$ ∴ total = $C$.

D – and E – calculate these yourself, but be careful.

**10**

**A** Capacitor 8.0 $\mu$F and p.d. 200 V so using $Q = VC$

$$Q = (200)(8.0 \times 10^{-6})$$
$$= 1600 \times 10^{-6} \text{ C.}$$

Capacitor 4.0 $\mu$F and p.d. 800 V so using $Q = VC$

$$Q = (800)(4.0 \times 10^{-6})$$
$$= 3200 \times 10^{-6} \text{ C.}$$

When connected, total charge = $1600 \times 10^{-6}$ C + $3200 \times 10^{-6}$ C
$$= 4800 \times 10^{-6} \text{ C.}$$

Since the capacitors are connected in parallel total capacitance is 12.0 $\mu$F.

So to find new p.d. use $Q = VC$     ∴ $V = 4800 \times 10^{-6}/12.0 \times 10^{-6}$ C
$$= 400 \text{ V.}$$

# Test 15

## Radioactivity

## Section 1: Short Questions

**ANSWER**

**1**

**(a)** $^{226}_{88}\text{Ra} \rightarrow \ ^{222}_{86}\text{Rn} + $ another particle

What numbers balance the top numbers (nucleon numbers), and the bottom numbers (proton numbers)?

$^{226}_{88}\text{Ra} \rightarrow \ ^{222}_{86}\text{Rn} + \ ^{4}_{2}\alpha$

i.e. an alpha particle is emitted.

**(b)** The experiment must show that alpha particles are emitted.
Choose an experiment which shows one of the properties of alpha particles, e.g. that they are stopped by paper.

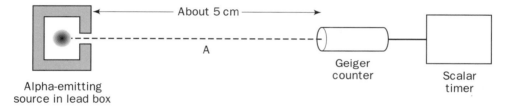

About 5 cm

A

Alpha-emitting source in lead box

Geiger counter

Scalar timer

Without the source, record the background count (over 5 minutes).
With source in position, record count rate $C_1$ (over 5 minutes).
Place paper at A and record count rate $C_2$ (over 5 minutes).
Since $C_2 \ll C_1$ the radiation is probably alpha particles.
$C_2$ will be close in magnitude to the background count.

**(c)** $N = N_0 e^{-\lambda t}$ and $\ln N = \ln N_0 - \lambda t$.
Since the half-life $(T_h)$ of radium is $1.6 \times 10^3$ years
and $\lambda = \ln 2/T_h$
$\quad \lambda = \ln 2/1.6 \times 10^3$
$\quad\quad = 4.33 \times 10^{-4} \ \text{year}^{-1}$.

Take $N_0 = 100$ and use the above equation

$\ln N = \ln(100) - (4.33 \times 10^{-4})(1.0 \times 10^3)$
$\quad\quad = 4.61 - 0.43$
$\quad\quad = 4.18$
$\quad N = 65\%$.

This is the number of atoms left.

Fraction of atoms decayed is 35%.

**2**

Half-life of a radioactive nuclide is the average time taken for half the atoms of the named nuclide to decay.

$$\text{Half-life } T_h = \frac{\ln 2}{\lambda} \qquad \text{where } \lambda \text{ is the decay constant}$$

$$\text{Since } N = N_0 e^{-\lambda t}$$
$$A_d = A_0 e^{-\lambda t}$$
$$\ln(A_d) = \ln(A_0) - \lambda t$$

A graph of $\ln(A_d)$ against $t$ will have

$$\text{slope} = -\lambda$$
$$y \text{ intercept} = \ln A_0$$

(a) To find initial activity read the $y$ intercept

$$y \text{ intercept} = 6.0 = \ln A_0$$
$$A_0 = 403 \text{ counts per minute}$$
$$A_0 = 403/60 \text{ counts per second}$$
$$A_0 = 6.72 \text{ Bq.}$$

(b) To find the decay constant ($\lambda$)

Measure slope of graph

$$\text{Slope} = -\lambda = \frac{-(6.0 - 1.2)}{(5.8 - 0)} \text{ h}^{-1}$$
$$\lambda = 0.828 \text{ h}^{-1}$$
$$= \frac{0.828}{60} \text{ min}^{-1}$$
$$= 0.0138 \text{ min}^{-1}$$
$$= \frac{0.138}{60} \text{ s}^{-1}$$
$$= 2.3 \times 10^{-4} \text{ s}^{-1}.$$

**3**

(a) (i) Half-life of $^{14}C$ is $1.76 \times 10^{11}$ s

Decay constant $\lambda = \ln 2/\text{half-life}$
$$= 0.693/1.76 \times 10^{11}$$
$$= 3.93 \times 10^{-12} \text{ s}^{-1}.$$

(ii) We are given the decay rate $dN/dt$

$$dN/dt = |\lambda N|$$

$$255 = (3.93 \times 10^{-12}) N$$
$$N = 6.47 \times 10^{13} \text{ kg}^{-1}.$$

**(b)** 1  Radioactivity is a random process since we do not know which atom will decay next; but we can be sure (well almost!) that one of the atoms will decay.

In each second the actual number decaying will obviously not always be exactly the same, so 255 Bq is an average. Provided our sample is large enough, we can apply certain rules which seem to work!

2  So half-life is the average time taken for half the atoms of $^{14}$C to decay.

The average time for half the atoms of a $^{14}$C sample to decay is $1.76 \times 10^{11}$ s.

**ANSWER**

**4**

The formula given  $dN/dt = -\lambda N$  can be used directly.

$$dN/dt = 6.4 \times 10^3 \text{ s}^{-1} \text{ and } \lambda = 12.6 \times 10^{-3} \text{ s}^{-1}$$

Substitute  $N = 6.4 \times 10^3 \div 12.6 \times 10^{-3}$
$$= 5.1 \times 10^5 \text{ atoms.}$$

**5**

**(a)** An isotope is one form of a substance (like hydrogen in this equation).
To balance this reaction, the top numbers (nucleon numbers) have to agree on both sides and so do the bottom numbers (proton numbers).
Here the two nuclides of hydrogen would behave the same chemically but have different numbers of particles in the nucleus.
The two isotopes, i.e. $^2_1$H and $^3_1$H, have the same proton number (1) but different nucleon numbers (2 or 3). This means their nuclei have the same number of protons but different numbers of neutrons.

**(b)** The bottom numbers add up to the same value on both sides of the equation, i.e. $1 + 1 = 2 + 0$, showing charge is conserved.

**(c)** The top numbers add up to the same value also, i.e. $2 + 3 = 4 + 1$, showing the number of nucleons is conserved. (What is a nucleon?)

**(d)** Mass is not conserved. Mass and energy together are conserved. Some of the mass is converted into energy. Remember $\Delta E = \Delta mc^2$?

**6**

Radioactive material has an unstable nucleus. In an effort to become stable it emits, at random, some combination of particles from its nucleus. The particles emitted could be $\alpha$, $\beta$ or $\gamma$.

**(a)** An $\alpha$ particle is a helium nucleus. It therefore has mass and positive charge.

**(b)** A $\beta$ particle is an electron. It has a smaller mass and a negative charge.

**(c)** A $\gamma$ particle is not really a particle at all. It is a quantum of electromagnetic radiation. In the usual sense, it has no mass and no charge.

The experiment is well described in textbooks, but notice the following points.
Your description must include:

A good labelled diagram.
A list of measurements to be made: 1 Background count.
                                       2 Count rate every 10 minutes.

Calculations                       Correct every reading for background.

Graph                                Plot corrected count rate $C$ against time.

Conclusion                       Use the graph to get at least two values of half-life,
e.g. time for $C$ to fall to $C/2$;
time for $C/2$ to fall to $C/4$.
Take an average of these values to find average half-life.

# Section 2: Multiple Choice

**A**   $^{214}_{82}\text{Pb} \rightarrow {}^{0}_{-1}\beta + {}^{0}_{0}\gamma + {}^{214}_{83}\text{X}$

To balance this reaction the top numbers (nucleon numbers) have to agree on both sides and so do the bottom numbers (proton numbers).
Hence the resultant nucleus is $^{214}_{83}\text{X}$
This has 83 protons and $(214 - 83) = 131$ neutrons.

## 2

**B**   This refers to the mass–energy relationship.
$E$ is energy released for a decrease $(m)$ in mass, while $c$ is speed of light in a vacuum.
$E = mc^2$
$E = (8.8 \times 10^{-30})(3.0 \times 10^8)^2$      $E = 7.92 \times 10^{-13}$ J.

**E**   Decay constant $= \dfrac{0.693}{\text{half-life}}$

$= \dfrac{0.693}{10}$

$= 0.0693 \text{ h}^{-1}.$

Radioactive sample obeys an exponential relationship.
If $N_0$ is the original number of atoms and $N$ is the number left not disintegrated after time $t$:

then          $N = N_0 e^{-\lambda t}$
$\ln N = \ln N_0 - \lambda t$
$\ln N = \ln(74 \times 10^{10}) - (0.0693)15$
$N = 2.6 \times 10^{11}.$

# Test 15

**4**

**E** Half-life $(T_h)$ = 20 days

Decay constant $(\lambda)$ = $\dfrac{\ln 2}{20}$ = 0.0347

If $N$ is the original number of atoms, then number left after time $t$ = $Ne^{-\lambda t}$.

Since the answer is given as a fraction:

number of atoms left after time $t$ = $\dfrac{1}{x}(N)$.

$\therefore \dfrac{N}{x} = Ne^{-\lambda t}$

$\dfrac{1}{x} = e^{-\lambda t}$

To find $x$ take logs

$\ln\left(\dfrac{1}{x}\right) = -\lambda t$

If $t$ = 100 days $\ln\left(\dfrac{1}{x}\right) = (0.0347)100 = -3.47$

$\dfrac{1}{x} = 0.0311$

$x = 32$.

**5**

**B** Total mass on left hand side = 14.011179 u.
Total mass on right hand side = (14.003074 + $x$).
Mass ($x$) is required to balance the equation.
According to Einstein, mass is equivalent to energy so energy must be emitted.

**6**

**A** Half-life = $\dfrac{\ln 2}{\text{decay constant}}$

= $\dfrac{0.693}{2.5 \times 10^{-7}}$

= $2.8 \times 10^6$ s.

**7**

**D** Let us see if the half-life is 1 minute.

|  | 2048 | counts/minute |
| 1 minute | | |
|  | 1024 | counts/minute |
| 1 minute | | |
|  | 512 | counts/minute |
| 1 minute | | |
|  | 256 | counts/minute |

Yes it is! Half-life *is* 1 minute!

After 4 minutes the count rate will be 256 ÷ 2.

*A-Level Physics: Structured Questions & Multiple Choice*                    **179**

**8**    **A**   The rate of decay is directly proportional to the number of nuclei present which have not yet decayed:

$$\frac{dN}{dt} \propto N.$$

**9**    **D**   Isotopes have the same proton numbers, but different nucleon numbers. Isotopes do not behave in the same radioactive way – they do behave the same chemically.

**10**    **D**   Two isotopes have the same proton number ($Z$) but different nucleon number.

$$_{Z}^{A}X \rightarrow _{Z}^{B}Y$$

The proton number must stay the same.

Consider D
$$_{2}^{4}\alpha + _{-1}^{0}\beta + _{-1}^{0}\beta$$

The proton number is not affected. An isotope of the original will be formed. Check the other answers to eliminate them.

# Test 16

## Atomic processes

### Section 1: Short Questions

**ANSWER**

**1**

The electron beam (equivalent to an electric current) will experience a force due to the magnetic field. This force will be perpendicular to the electron beam (by Fleming's left-hand rule) and will push the electrons into a circular path.

**(a)** Force due to the magnetic field causing circular path

$$= (B)(\text{charge on electron})(\text{speed of electron})$$

$$\frac{mv^2}{r} = Bev$$

We want to find the kinetic energy $(\frac{1}{2}mv^2)$

From above $\quad mv^2 = rBev$

Therefore $\quad \frac{1}{2}mv^2 = \frac{1}{2}(rBev)$

Kinetic energy $\quad = \frac{1}{2}(0.048)(1.4 \times 10^{-3})(1.6 \times 10^{-19})(1.2 \times 10^{7})$
in joules $\qquad = 6.45 \times 10^{-17}$ J

Kinetic energy in eV $\quad = \dfrac{(6.45 \times 10^{-17})}{1.6 \times 10^{-19}} = 4.03 \times 10^{2}$ eV.

**(b)** The proton has a much larger mass than the electron, but the same magnitude of charge. From the above, the kinetic energy of the electron is about 400 eV, but the kinetic energy of protons is about $500 \times 10^{9}$ eV. The protons have a very high velocity.

From the above $\dfrac{mv^2}{r} = Bqv$ ($q$ is charge on proton)

$$mv^2 = Bqvr$$

$$r = mv/Bq.$$

If $B$ and $q$ are the same as above but $m$ and $v$ are much larger, $r$ will have to be large as well.

**2**

Read this question very carefully. The ionisation energy is the energy required to lift an electron from ground state to infinity (where the nucleus no longer exerts a force on the electron). The excitation energy is the energy required to lift an electron to the new level.

Ionisation energy of hydrogen is 13.6 eV. This means that 13.6 eV of energy are required to lift an electron from the ground state to the zero energy level. The first excitation energy is 10.2 eV. This means that 10.2 eV of energy are required to lift an electron from the ground state to the first energy level. These movements are shown on the diagram.

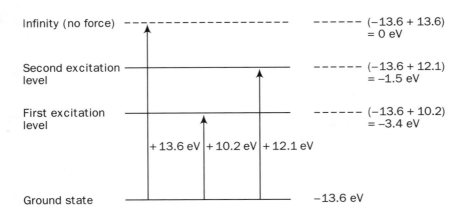

So the diagram required is:

The longest wavelength will result from the smallest energy jump, i.e. $(E_2 - E_1)$

$$(E_2 - E_1) = hc/\lambda$$
$$\lambda = hc/(E_2 - E_1)$$
$$= (6.6 \times 10^{-34})(3 \times 10^8)/(3.4 - 1.5)(1.6 \times 10^{-19})$$
$$= 6.5 \times 10^{-7} \text{ m.}$$

**ANSWER**

**3**

By the quantum theory, energy exists in small packets called 'quanta'. Each quantum in a wave of frequency ($f$) contains the same amount of energy ($E$).

$E = hf$     $h$ is called Planck's constant.

So for $\gamma$ wave        $E = 2 \times 10^{-11}$ J     $f = \dfrac{2 \times 10^{-11}}{h}$

and for radio wave     $E_R = 6 \times 10^{-28}$ J     $f_R = \dfrac{6 \times 10^{-28}}{h}$.

Hence:
Frequency of radio wave < frequency of $\gamma$ wave;
Energy per quantum of radio wave < energy per quantum of $\gamma$ wave.

**4**

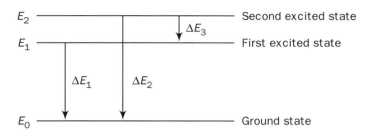

**(a)** Since $\Delta E = hc/\lambda$

$\Delta E_1 = (6.63 \times 10^{-34})(3.00 \times 10^8)/(121.5 \times 10^{-9})$

$= 1.64 \times 10^{-18}$ J

$\Delta E_2 = (6.63 \times 10^{-34})(3.00 \times 10^8)/(102.5 \times 10^{-9})$

$= 1.94 \times 10^{-18}$ J.

**(b)**

$\Delta E_3 = \Delta E_2 - \Delta E_1$

$= (1.94 \times 10^{-18}) - (1.64 \times 10^{-18})$

$= 0.30 \times 10^{-18}$ J.

To calculate the required wavelength use

$\Delta E_3 = hc/\lambda_3$

$\lambda_3 = hc/\Delta E_3$

$= (6.63 \times 10^{-34})(3.00 \times 10^8)/(0.30 \times 10^{-18})$

$= 6.63 \times 10^{-7}$ m

$= 663$ nm.

**5**

The apparatus is shown below.

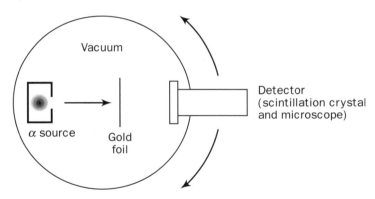

Very thin gold foil was bombarded with $\alpha$ particles. These were expected to go straight through, since they were travelling at high speeds. The $\alpha$ particles were detected after they passed through the foil. The angles through which they were deflected were measured together with the frequency at which they occurred.

The main conclusions were:

1   Since most of the $\alpha$ particles passed straight through, the gold foil must contain a lot of empty space.

2   Some of the $\alpha$ particles were deflected through quite large angles – they must be pushed off their path by another positive charge ($\alpha$ is positive).

3   A few of the α particles were deflected so much that they returned along the same path. The positive charge in the gold foil must be very large and probably linked with a relatively large mass.

4   Hence the main conclusion – that the centre of the gold atom has a large mass and large positive charge compared with the α particles.

**ANSWER**

**6**

(a) The photoelectric effect occurs when light falls on a metal surface and electrons are emitted. The wavelength of the light is very important. It must be shorter than a certain value, called the threshold wavelength, which is different for different metals. In other words, the threshold wavelength is the longest wavelength that allows the emission of electrons.

The work function is the smallest energy required to just emit electrons from the metal surface.

(b) Energy in incident quantum of light $E$ is used to overcome the work function $W$ and to supply energy to the emitted electrons $K$.

$$E = W + K$$
$$hc/\lambda = W + K$$
$$\therefore W = hc/\lambda - K$$
$$W = \frac{(6.6 \times 10^{-34})(3.0 \times 10^{8})}{5.0 \times 10^{-7}} - (2.4 \times 10^{-19})$$

What do you get for $W$? ($1.6 \times 10^{-19}$ J).

(c) Use the same formula again.
This time   $hc/\lambda = 1.6 \times 10^{-19} + 9.0 \times 10^{-19} = 10.6 \times 10^{-19}$
$$\lambda = hc/10.6 \times 10^{-19}$$
$$= \frac{(6.6 \times 10^{-34})(3.0 \times 10^{8})}{10.6 \times 10^{-19}}$$
$$= 1.9 \times 10^{-7} \text{ m}.$$

**7**

Experiment required – create a thin oil film on water using apparatus below.

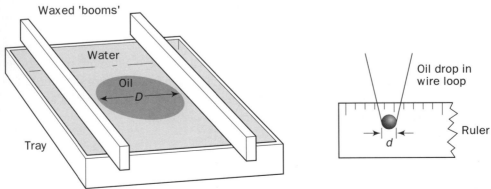

1   A waxed tray is filled right to the top with water and carefully levelled.
2   The two waxed booms are placed in the centre and then slowly drawn to the outside in order to clean the surface.

3   The surface of the water is sprinkled with lycopodium powder.

4   A small oil drop is picked up in a loop of fine wire, viewed through a lens, and its diameter ($d$) measured against a scale.

5   The oil drop is placed into the centre of the water. The oil spreads rapidly to a patch of diameter ($D$) measured with a ruler.

6   Repeat the experiment and get average values for $d$ and $D$.

7   Calculate volume $V$ of oil drop using $V = (4/3)\pi r^3$ where $r = d/2$, assuming the drop is a sphere.

8   Calculate volume $V$ of oil film (same as above) using $V = \pi h (D/2)^2$ where $h$ is thickness of oil film.

9   Equate the equations from 7 and 8 above to find $h$.

10  It is assumed that $h$ is the diameter of one oil molecule, or the oil film is one molecule thick.

Has this question been answered?

(a) See diagram above.
(b) Measurements – see 4 and 5 above.
(c) Calculation – see 7, 8 and 9.
(d) See 10.

# Section 2: Multiple Choice

**ANSWER**

**1**

A   Planck's constant   $h = \dfrac{E}{f}$

$$h = \dfrac{J}{Hz}$$

$$h = J\,s$$

$$h = N\,m\,s$$

Which answer has these units?

**2**

A   Einstein's photoelectric equation quotes
$$E = E_0 + \tfrac{1}{2}mv^2$$
where $E$   is the energy of the incident quantum;

$E_0$   is the work function (i.e. the minimum energy required to release an electron);

$\tfrac{1}{2}mv^2$   is the kinetic energy of the released electron if there is any extra energy available.

The answer required here is the magnitude of $E$ since there is no energy left over to give to the electron.

Energy in incident quantum:
$$E = E_0 = hc/\lambda$$
$$= \frac{(6.6 \times 10^{-34})}{7.0 \times 10^{-7}}(3 \times 10^8)$$
$$= 2.8 \times 10^{-19} \text{ J.}$$

**3**

**E** In the photoelectric effect electrons are emitted provided there is enough energy in the incident quantum. Then, if there is enough energy, we get one electron for every quantum. The rate at which electrons are emitted will depend on the number of quanta every second. The brighter the light, the bigger this will be.

**4**

**B** Make sure you understand the principles of this experiment. You are told that most of the alpha particles pass through with very little deflection. So the deduction from that information is the answer.

**5**

**E** For an electron (charge $q$, mass $m$, velocity $v$) moving in a magnetic field (flux density $B$)

$$\text{Centripetal force } \frac{mv^2}{r} = Bqv$$

$$\frac{mv}{Bq} = R.$$

The effect of the constant force in direct opposition to its motion will be to decrease the velocity. If the velocity decreases continually then $R$ will decrease also.

**6**

**D** Energy change between the given levels:

$$
\begin{aligned}
E &= -3.7 - (-10.4) \text{ eV} \\
&= 6.7 \text{ eV} \\
&= 6.7 \times 1.6 \times 10^{-19} \text{ J} \\
E &= \frac{hc}{\lambda}
\end{aligned}
$$

$$6.7 \times 1.6 \times 10^{-19} = \frac{(6.6 \times 10^{-34})(3 \times 10^8)}{\lambda}$$

$$\therefore \lambda = 1.8 \times 10^{-7} \text{ m.}$$

**7**

**B** The yellow light has less energy per quantum than blue light. (The wavelength of yellow light is longer than that of blue light.) If blue light only just causes electrons to be emitted, then the yellow light will not have enough energy to cause this effect at all.

**8**

**B** The magnetic effect on a stream of charged particles can be explained using Fleming's left hand rule.

First finger     – magnetic field (north to south)
Second finger   – conventional current (i.e. opposite way to electron flow)
Thumb           – direction of the force

Try it!

**ANSWER**

**9**

**B** This is about the photoelectric effect. If the intensity of the radiation is halved, the number of photons (quanta) of energy will be halved. Since one photon causes one electron to be emitted, this means the *number* of electrons will be halved.

NB The velocity and energy of the electrons depends on the wavelength of the radiation, not on its intensity.

**10**

**A** Since blue light has a *shorter* wavelength than red light, the energy per quantum of blue light is larger. A smaller energy jump will give rise to a quantum of red light.

## Section 1: Short Questions

**ANSWER 1**

(a) Electric potential difference = energy transfer ÷ charge

$$1 \text{ volt} = \frac{1 \text{ joule}}{1 \text{ coulomb}}$$

$$= \frac{(\text{newton})(\text{metre})}{(\text{amp})(\text{seconds})}$$

$$= \frac{(\text{kg} \times \text{m s}^{-2})(\text{m})}{(\text{A})(\text{s})}$$

$$= \text{kg m}^2 \text{ A}^{-1} \text{ s}^{-3}.$$

Make sure you know which units are BASE UNITS.

(b) Homogeneity in an equation is demonstrated by having the same units on both sides.

Consider $P = V^2/R$

L.H.S.  $P$  →  watts  →  joules/second  →  $J s^{-1}$

R.H.S.  $\dfrac{V^2}{R}$  →  $\dfrac{(\text{volts})^2}{\text{ohms}}$

→  $\dfrac{(\text{volts})(\text{volts})}{\text{volts/amps}}$

→  $(\text{volts})(\text{amps})$

→  $\dfrac{(\text{joules})}{(\text{coulombs})} \times \dfrac{(\text{coulombs})}{(\text{seconds})}$

→  $\dfrac{\text{joules}}{\text{seconds}}$         →  $J s^{-1}$

Hence L.H.S. = R.H.S.
So equation is homogeneous.

**ANSWER**

**2**

Power = work done/time taken to do the work

Power = $J s^{-1}$

$= N m s^{-1}$

$= (kg\, m\, s^{-2})(m)(s^{-1})$

$= kg\, m^2\, s^{-3}$

These are all base units (what are the others?).

Power is scalar.

Power has magnitude only – no direction.

**3**

Do you know which are the base units? Learn them!

$$F = \frac{Q_1 Q_2}{4\pi\varepsilon_0 r^2} \rightarrow \varepsilon_0 = \frac{Q_1 Q_2}{4\pi F r^2}$$

$$= C^2/(kg\, m\, s^{-2})(m^2)$$

$$= C^2\, kg^{-1}\, m^{-3}\, s^2$$

Then for $c^2 = 1/\varepsilon_0 \mu_0$

L.H.S. = $(m\, s^{-1})^2 = m^2\, s^{-2}$

R.H.S. = $1/(C^2\, kg^{-1}\, m^{-3}\, s^2)(kg\, m\, C^{-2}) = m^2\, s^{-2}$

∴ Equation is homogeneous with respect to units.

**(a)** All equations must have the same units on both sides or they do not make sense, e.g. 1 kg is not equal to 1 $m^2$.

**(b)** If an equation includes a dimensionless constant, then this will not be included with the units, e.g. the area of a circle $= \pi r^2$ (units ignore $\pi$).

**4**

A vector quantity has magnitude and direction.

A scalar quantity has magnitude only.

Vector quantities: velocity, acceleration, displacement.

Scalar quantities: energy, power, distance.

Kinetic energy is scalar; it has no direction. However, momentum is a vector so, since the direction is changing, momentum is changing as well.

**5**

Each equation has to be investigated individually. Compare the units on the right hand side with those on the left.

You should find that **(b)** is correct.

The following graphs are required:

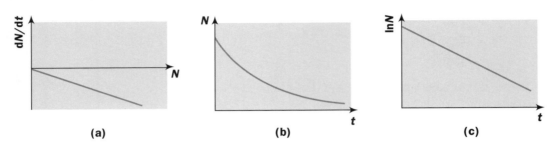

(a)                 (b)                 (c)

**(a)** Straight line through origin and slope $= -\lambda$    $(dN/dt \propto N)$.

**(b)** Not very easy to find $\lambda$ here.

**(c)** Another straight line with slope equal to $-\lambda$    $(\ln N = \ln N_0 - \lambda t)$.

Units of **(a)** $A$ are $m^2$, **(b)** $T_1^4$ are $K^4$ and **(c)** $\sigma$ – we need a calculation:

$$\sigma = W/A(T_1^4 - T_2^4)$$
$$= J\,s^{-1}/m^2\,K^4$$
$$= kg\,m^2\,s^{-3}/m^2\,K^4 = kg\,s^{-3}\,K^{-4}$$

$$W = \sigma A(T_1^4 - T_2^4)$$
Remove brackets
$$W = \sigma A T_1^4 - \sigma A T_2^4$$
$$(y = mx + c).$$

Graph will be linear. To find $\sigma$ measure the slope and divide by $A$.

# Section 2: Multiple Choice

## 1

**A**   Specific heat capacity is defined as the energy required to raise the temperature of 1 kg of a material through $1°C$ (or 1 K)

i.e.    $(J)(kg^{-1})(K^{-1})$
or     $(N\,m)(kg^{-1})(K^{-1})$       since $J = N\,m$
or     $(kg\,ms^{-2})(m)(kg^{-1})(K^{-1})$    since $N = kg\,m\,s^{-2}$

Sort it out and we get $m^2 s^{-2} K^{-1}$.

**E**   Learn the base units.

NB   We want UNITS not QUANTITIES.

1 volt $=$ 1 joule/coulomb.
The volt is a *derived* unit, not a base unit.

**ANSWER**

**3**

**E**  Find a formula with Planck's constant ($h$) in it, for example,

$$E = hf$$

where $E$ is energy (J);
$f$ is frequency (Hz or $s^{-1}$).

Hence $h = E/f$
$\phantom{Hence\ h} = J/s^{-1}$
$\phantom{Hence\ h} = J\,s$
$\phantom{Hence\ h} = N\,m\,s$
$\phantom{Hence\ h} = (kg\,m\,s^{-2})m\,s$
$\phantom{Hence\ h} = kg\,m^2\,s^{-1}.$

**4**

**E**  Density $= \dfrac{X}{force}$

$X = (density)(force)$
$\phantom{X} = (kg\,m^{-3})(kg\,m\,s^{-2})$
$\phantom{X} = kg\,m^{-2}\,s^{-2}.$

**5**

**B**  Learn the base units!
The base units involved in this type of question are:
metre;
kilogram;
second;
ampère;
mole;
Kelvin.

**6**

**B**  Consider A   Magnetic flux density   $B = \dfrac{\mu_0 I}{2\pi y}$

$\phantom{Consider A Magnetic flux density}B \propto 1/y$

Consider B   Electric field strength   $E = \dfrac{q}{4\pi\varepsilon y^2}$

$\phantom{Consider B Electric field strength}E \propto 1/y^2$

Consider C   Electric field strength   $E = \dfrac{V}{d}$

$\phantom{Consider C Electric field strength}E \propto 1/y$

Consider D   Magnetic flux density   $B = \dfrac{\mu_0 I n}{L}$

$\phantom{Consider D Magnetic flux density}B \propto y$

Consider E   (Hooke's Law)   Load $F = ky$

$\phantom{Consider E (Hooke's Law) Load}F \propto y$

Test 17

**7**    **B**   This is a definition you should know.

1 volt = 1 joule/coulomb

NB   1 coulomb/second = 1 ampère
1 joule/second = 1 watt.

**8**    **C**

$$E = a\theta + b\theta^2$$

Divide by $\theta$    $\dfrac{E}{\theta} = a + b\theta$

Compare with   y $= c + mx$   (straight line equation)
Slope ($m$)     $= +b.$

**9**    **C**   Energy ($E$) of a photon

$$E = \frac{hc}{\lambda}$$   where $h$ and $c$ are constant and $\lambda$ is a wavelength

If $E = p$    and    $\lambda = q$

$$p = \frac{hc}{q}$$

$$p = \frac{constant}{q}.$$

**10**    **C**   Energy, speed, work, distance and temperature are all scalar quantities.
Force, velocity, acceleration and momentum are all vector quantities.

# Section 1: Short Questions

**ANSWER**

**1**

A free-body diagram shows all the forces acting on the ball (it does not show forces acting on anything else).

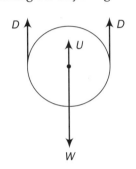

*W* weight (equal to the gravitational pull of the earth on the ball).

*U* upthrust (equal to the weight of the oil displaced by the ball). This is caused by a difference in pressure above and below the ball.

*D* viscous drag (equal to frictional force between the surface of the ball and the oil). This is due to the movement of the ball through the oil.

NB In this type of question forces must be drawn from the point where they act, not 'floating about'! When describing what is happening, do not discuss 'the body' and 'the liquid'. This question is about a ball in oil. Use the words 'ball' and 'oil'.

**2**

This lamp has a normal operating voltage of 12 V and when used in this way the lamp's power is 24 W. The current through it will be 2 A ($IV = 24$) and its resistance will be 6 $\Omega$ ($V = IR$). All this is only true if the p.d. across the lamp is 12 V.

**(a)** Look at the 12 V, 4.00 A reading.
With the 12 V across the lamp we expect a 2 A reading, so the rest of the current must flow through the resistor; lamp and resistors are in parallel.
(If the resistor was in series with the lamp, then the current would be less than 2 A.)

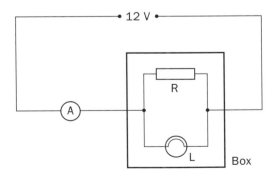

**(b)** From above, 2 A flows through the lamp. 2 A flows through R, so R and lamp have the same resistance of 6 $\Omega$.

**(c)** When 1.0 V is applied the current is 1.17 A.

Total resistance in box $= 1.0/1.17 = 0.8\ \Omega$.

For parallel resistors

$$\frac{1}{R_{\text{TOTAL}}} = \frac{1}{R_{\text{LAMP}}} + \frac{1}{R}$$

$$\frac{1}{0.8} = \frac{1}{R_{\text{LAMP}}} + \frac{1}{6}$$

$$R_{\text{LAMP}} = 1\ \Omega \text{ (lamp is cold, resistance low)}$$

$$\text{Percentage increase} = \frac{(6-1)100}{1} = 500\%.$$

**(d)** 24 V is a lot for a 12 V lamp. The lamp has blown. All current now passes through R.

$$R = \frac{V}{I} = \frac{24}{4} = 6\ \Omega.$$

**ANSWER**

**3**

**(a)** When two electrostatic charges approach one another then Coulomb's Law will apply.

$$F = \frac{1}{4\pi\epsilon}\frac{q_1 q_2}{r^2}$$

$q_1$ = charge on $\alpha$ particle $= +(2)(1.6 \times 10^{-19})$ C

$q_2$ = charge on gold nucleus $= +(79)(1.6 \times 10^{-19})$ C

$$F = \left(\frac{1}{4\pi \times 8.85 \times 10^{-12}}\right)\left(\frac{2 \times 1.6 \times 10^{-19} \times 79 \times 1.6 \times 10^{-19}}{s^2}\right)$$

$$F = \frac{3.64 \times 10^{-26}}{s^2}$$

**(b)**

Electric potential energy $= Fs$

Initial kinetic energy

of $\alpha$ particle in joules = electric p.e. at impact

Kinetic energy of particle $= 1.8$ MeV $= 1.8 \times 1.6 \times 10^{-19} \times 10^6$ J

$(1.8 \times 1.6 \times 10^{-19} \times 10^6) = Fs$

$2.88 \times 10^{-13} = Fs$

Substitute for $F$ from above

$$2.88 \times 10^{-13} = \frac{(3.64 \times 10^{-26})}{s^2} \times s$$

$$s = \frac{(3.64 \times 10^{-26})}{2.88 \times 10^{-13}}$$

$$= 1.26 \times 10^{-13}\,\text{m}.$$

Of course $s$ is very small – but relate this to the question ($s$ is atomic size).

$s$ = radius of $\alpha$ particle + radius of gold nucleus (approximately).

**ANSWER**

**4**

Vertical wires

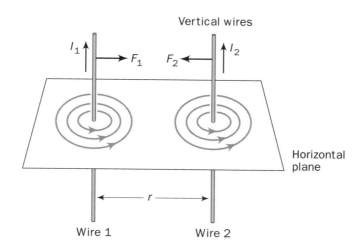

Horizontal plane

Wire 1    Wire 2

Each wire generates its own magnetic field (by right-hand corkscrew rule). Each wire is situated in the magnetic field of the other.
Hence by Fleming's left hand rule the force on wire 1 is to the right ($F_1$).
The force of wire 2 is to the left ($F_2$).
So the wires attract one another ($F_1 = F_2$).

The ampère is defined as the current that flows in each of two wires and produces a force between the wires of $2 \times 10^{-7}$ newtons per metre.
(These wires are infinitely long, straight, parallel, of negligible cross-section and placed 1 metre apart in a vacuum.)

**5**

(a) The total sum of energy in the universe remains constant. To state this principle in another way, the total energy in a closed system remains constant. Energy is not lost or gained – it just changes from one form to another.

(b) Energy is measured in joules. One joule is the amount of energy gained when a force of one newton moves its point of application through one metre.

(c) Electrical output required is $2.00 \times 10^9$ W, and 600 W m$^{-2}$ arrive. Only 20% is available.
∴ 20% of 600 W m$^{-2}$ is 120 W m$^{-2}$.
Output $2.00 \times 10^9$ W required and 120 W m$^{-2}$ arriving means area required
$= 2.00 \times 10^9$ W/120 W m$^{-2}$ $= 1.7 \times 10^7$ m$^2$. (Is this large?)

**6**

(a) Step index fibre has a core in the centre and cladding round the outside as shown in the diagram.

**Refractive index *n***

There is a sudden change in refractive index between the core and the cladding, with the core having a much larger value. This means that total internal reflection occurs in the core and light can travel down the core with hardly any loss in energy.

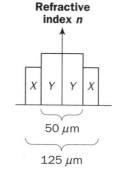

$X$ | $Y$ | $Y$ | $X$

50 μm

125 μm

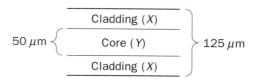

50 μm { Cladding (X)

Core (Y)  } 125 μm

Cladding (X)

**(b)** A pulse of light will contain many different wavelengths. Each wavelength travels at a different speed so will arrive at a different time, e.g. blue light will take longer than red. Thus a pulse sent into the fibre will come out wider.
This is called material dispersion. Calculation:

$$\text{velocity} = \text{distance/time}$$
$$\text{time} = \text{distance/velocity}$$

$\therefore$ We know the distance. Can we find the velocity?

$$\text{Definition of refractive index } n = \frac{\text{speed of light in vacuum}}{\text{speed of light in medium}}$$

Since the light travels down the core
For core $\quad\quad\quad\quad\quad\quad n = 3.0 \times 10^8/v$, so $v = 3.0 \times 10^8/1.5$
$$= 2.0 \times 10^8 \text{ m s}^{-1}$$
From above $\quad\quad\quad$ Time $= 20/2.0 \times 10^8 \quad = 10^{-9}$ s or 1 ns

**ANSWER**

**7**

Wave-particle duality refers to the theory of waves.
Waves can be explained in two ways:

(i) As a continuous advance of energy where
Intensity $\propto$ (amplitude)$^2$

or

(ii) As a series of packets of energy (particles of energy) called quanta or photons.
Each quantum (or photon) in the same wave has an identical amount of energy ($E$),

where $E = hf$;
$\quad h$ is Planck's constant;
$\quad f$ is frequency of the wave.


# Section 2: Multiple Choice

**1**

**B** The best way to tackle this one is to make some calculations.
If $I$ is the current flowing,
the power generated in $R$  Power $= I^2R$
$$\text{But} \quad\quad E = I(R + r)$$
$$\frac{E}{(R + r)} = I$$
Power generated in $R = I^2R = \{E/(R+ r)\}^2 \times R$

Use $R = 2\ \Omega$  Power generated $= \{6/(2 + 2)\}^2 \times 2 = 4.5$ W
Use $R = 3\ \Omega$  Power generated $= \{6/(3 + 2)\}^2 \times 3 = 4.3$ W  (i.e. $R$ is larger).
Use $R = 1\ \Omega$  Power generated $= \{6/(1 + 2)\}^2 \times 1 = 4.0$ W  (i.e. $R$ is smaller).
The largest amount of power is generated when $R = r$.

ANSWER

**2**  **E**  A force of 10 N applied for 2 s produces an impulse (force × time) which causes a change in momentum of the mass.

In the usual notation
$$Ft = mv - mu$$
$$(10)\,(2) = (5)\,(v) - (5)(0)$$
$$4 \text{ m s}^{-1} = v.$$

**3**  **E**  There is no force applied from $t = 2$ s to $t = 3$ s.
There will be no acceleration during this time. The velocity will stay constant at $4 \text{ m s}^{-1}$. When the new force is applied for 1 s it will cause a change in momentum (new momentum $mv$).
$$Ft = mv - mu$$
$$(10)\,(1) = (5)(v) - (5)(4)$$
$$v = 6 \text{ m s}^{-1}$$

**4**  **D**  Height of liquid × density × $g$

$$\rightarrow (\text{m}) \times (\text{kg m}^{-3}) \times (\text{m s}^{-2})$$
$$\rightarrow \text{kg m}^{-1}\,\text{s}^{-2}$$
$$\rightarrow (\text{kg m s}^{-2})\,\text{m}^{-2}$$
$$\rightarrow \text{N m}^{-2}$$

or perhaps you know this formula gives pressure?

**5**  **C**  Gravitational field strength is defined as the force acting on a mass of 1 kg, i.e. N kg$^{-1}$.

**6**  **C**  The kinetic energy of the car is converted into heat.

$$\text{Kinetic energy} = \tfrac{1}{2}mv^2 = 500 \times 10^3$$
$$(\tfrac{1}{2})(1500)v^2 = 500 \times 10^3$$
$$v^2 = \frac{(2)(500 \times 10^3)}{1500}$$
$$v = 25.8 \text{ m s}^{-1}.$$

**7**  **C**  $\gamma$ is the most penetrating (not stopped in air).
$\beta$ is the next penetrating (several metres in air).
$\alpha$ does not get very far (a few centimetres).

**ANSWER**

**8**

A  Transition $E_3 \rightarrow E_2$

Energy emitted $= E_3 - E_2 = \dfrac{hc}{2.4 \times 10^{-7}}$

Transition $E_2 \rightarrow E_1$

Energy emitted $= E_2 - E_1 = \dfrac{hc}{10.0 \times 10^{-8}}$

Transition $E_3 \rightarrow E_1$

Energy emitted $= (E_3 - E_2) + (E_2 - E_1) = \dfrac{hc}{2.4 \times 10^{-7}} + \dfrac{hc}{10.0 \times 10^{-8}}$

If the new wavelength $= \lambda$   $\dfrac{hc}{\lambda} = \dfrac{hc}{2.4 \times 10^{-7}} + \dfrac{hc}{10.0 \times 10^{-8}}$

$\dfrac{1}{\lambda} = \dfrac{1}{2.4 \times 10^{-7}} + \dfrac{1}{10.0 \times 10^{-8}}$

$= (0.42 \times 10^7) + (0.10 \times 10^8)$
$= 1.42 \times 10^7$

$\lambda = \dfrac{1}{1.42 \times 10^7}$

$= 0.7 \times 10^{-7}$
$= 7.0 \times 10^{-8}$ m.

**9**

A  Rate of flow of energy $= $ J s$^{-1}$.
Rate of flow of charge $= $ C s$^{-1}$.
These are equivalent, all the others are wrong. Which did you choose?
Thermal energy moves and charge moves. Thermal conductivity is equivalent to electrical conductivity (conductivity is the reciprocal of resistivity).
Temperature difference is equivalent to potential difference.

**10**

A  Consider these answers in reverse order.
   E  The elastic limit has not been reached, so wire has not reached the yield point.
   D  Tensile stress is force/area so not dependent on length.
   C  As seen in D the length is not involved.
   B  This is not the definition of Young's modulus.
   A  The wire itself does have mass, so each part of the wire will be pulled by those parts below as well as by the load. The extension of each part of the wire will increase the further you get from the point of suspension.